SF

LA

graphic
design:

CALIFORNIA

ISBN 0-942604-56-3
Library of Congress Catalog Card Number 96-076797

Distributors to the trade in the United States and Canada:
Van Nostrand Reinhold, 115 Fifth Avenue, New York, NY 10003

Published by:
Madison Square Press
10 East 23rd Street, New York, NY 10010
Phone: (212) 505-0950
Fax: (212) 979-2207

Jacket Design / Divider Pages by Vrontikis Design

Design and Management of this book by Harish Patel Design

Printed in Hong Kong

TABLE OF CONTENTS

INTRODUCTION

Before World War II, the state of California was considered by many as a state balancing precariously on the western edge of the country. It had some industry, lots of movies, acres of agriculture, and the giant Redwoods. After the War, a mass migration started westward and it has yet to stop. It's been said, "The Rose Bowl has brought more people to California than the Greyhound." That may be true — something has helped make this state very different from the other 49.

With the migration came working people who got things started, who constructed, who explored. They tended to be entrepreneurial, risk-takers, innovative thinkers not part of the established businesses fed by old-world cultures way back East. These people settled in California to reinvent businesses and lifestyles, and to develop a true cultural diversity.

These very conditions have proven to be the best incubator for graphic designers. Over the decades since World War II, hundreds of graphic designers have either been born in California, trained there, or moved there from other parts of the country or the world to ply their trade with great success. Long a style center for graphics used in the movies, television, fashion, music and food industries, California graphic designers have also led the way in design, utilizing all of the new technologies.

The design firms selected to appear in this volume exemplify and embrace the great tradition of inventive problem solving, style setting, and the creative use of all the new technologies. The work shown by the design firms on these pages should be a true inspiration to all graphic designers everywhere.

The Publisher

adams/
morioka
inc.

LA

Clarity, purity, honesty and resonance are the ideals that drive all work at Adams Morioka, Inc. These concepts came about as a clear reaction to the complexity, confusion, and dilution of message prevelant in graphic design. "It was either clean it up and make the world a better place," says partner Sean Adams, "or become a monorail driver in Tomorrowland." Noreen Morioka agrees. "Everything was all so muddy. Somehow in the last 20 years, the idea that design had to be weird and unintelligible was tied to it being good."

The concept of collaboration also plays a large part in all Adams Morioka projects. Not only collaboration between the two principals, Sean Adams and Noreen Morioka, and other designers in the firm, but also collaborations with clients and experts in other mediums. This "virtual office" concept has allowed the firm to complete work as diverse as corporate identity programs for multi-national corporations, videos, web sites, large scale environmental graphics, interiors and packaging.

Their commitment to cleaning away the tricks and "40,000 boxes" and paring communication down to its most direct and thoughtful level is counterpointed by their reputation as the "friendly alternative." As one of their clients recently said, "Adams Morioka, Inc: Where the fun never stops!"

10

Photo: Blake Little

THE AMERICAN ACADEMY OF ARTS AND SCIENCES
THE GETTY CENTER FOR THE HISTORY OF ART AND THE HUMANITIES
THE UNIVERSITY OF CALIFORNIA HUMANITIES RESEARCH INSTITUTE PRESENT

CENSORSHIP +

SILENCING

PRACTICES OF CULTURAL REGULATION

1

1

1. *Poster for The Getty Center for the History of Art and the Humanities.*

2. *Advertisement for SEE, a production company.*

3. *Poster for the Slamdance film festival.*

4. *Poster for an APLA benefit.*

5. *Poster for American Institute of Architects.*

6. *Poster for LA Louver Gallery.*

SLAMDANCE

WHERE THE WILDERNESS MEETS THE GARDEN

SLAMDANCE INTERNATIONAL FILM FESTIVAL · JANUARY 19-25, 1996 · PARK CITY · UTAH

1

totally cupid

a valentine's tribute to love and fashion

Tuesday, February 14, 1995
6:30 p.m.
Pacific Design Center
The Gallery, Floor 5 Blue

$50 General Admission
$60 At-the-Door
$125 VIP Admission, including
VIP Reception hosted by the
PDC President, Andrew Wolf.
Join honored guests in the
extraordinary new PDC Idea
House.

Parking is available in the
Pacific Design Center parking
structure. Please use
San Vicente Boulevard entrance.

For VIP ticket holders, please
give your name to the attendant
at the parking structure.

Tickets are available for
purchase through APLA by
phoning 213.993.1564

PRESENTED BY AIDS PROJECT LOS ANGELES

2

ANNUAL DESIGN AWARDS 1994

AIA/LA

JURY: ZAHA HADID   GARY LEE   WES JONES   KEVIN STARR

5

Ed Moses

PAINT

Tony Berlant *Recent Miracles*

6

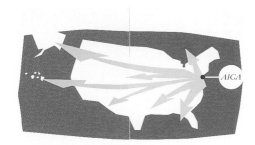

12

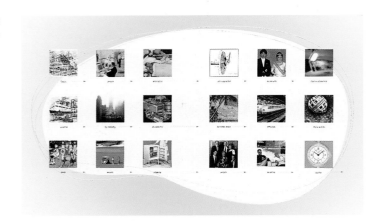

2

1

1. Introduction spreads for
   Wired magazine.

2. Spreads for AIGA Capital Campaign
   booklet.

3. Design for architectural book.

4. Poster for Southern California
   Institute of Architecture.

5. Poster for American Institute of
   Graphic Arts.

6. Promotional calendar for
   Adams Morioka, Inc.

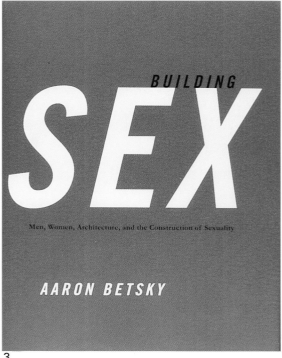

3

4

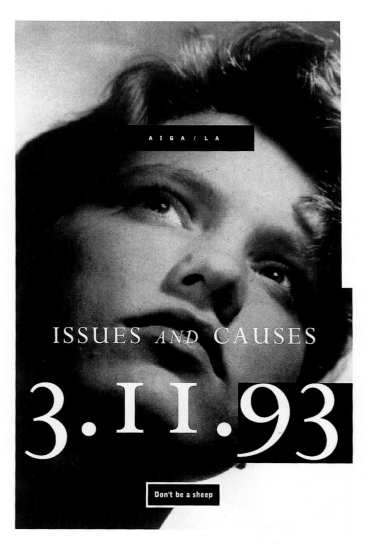

5

Rodeo Roundup

Hawaiian Getaway!

14

1

2

3

5

6

1. *Fusion restaurant interiors,
   color, materials.*

2. *Fusion restaurant menu,
   take-out items.*

3. *Fusion restaurant dinnerware.*

4. *Pacific Design Center signage.*

5. *Fusion entrance signage.*

6. *Ahmanson Theater signage program.*

1. *Virtual logo for a design center.*
2. *Identity of an APLA benefit.*
3. *Identity of a landscape architecture firm.*
4. *Identity for AIGA newsletter (voice of...).*
5. *Identity for alternative film festival.*
6. *Identity for interiors showhouse.*
7. *Identity for medical corporation.*
8. *Identity for printing company.*
9. *Identity for restaurant.*
10. *Masthead for magazine.*
11. *Identity for alternative film organization.*
12. *Identity for gallery.*

1

2

ah'bé
Calvin Abe • Landscape Architecture

3

4

5

6

7

8

9

De•SiGN MaTTeRs

10

11

12

ADAMS MORIOKA, INC.

(at press time. Adams Morioka, Inc. has merged with Maddocks & Company(

2011 Pontius Avenue, Los Angeles, CA 90025   310.477.4227   Fax: 310.479.5767

1. *Edge Television network design.*

2. *A+M Records promo video (Dayton Faris: directors).*

3. *Experimental film documentary titles for PBS.*

4. *Experimental film documentary leaders for PBS.*

5. *REM Monster Tour documetary (Dayton Faris: directors).*

6. *Interactive television program for Maverick Productions (Dayton Faris: directors).*

16

1

2

3

4

5

6

kimberly
baer
design

LA

18

Kimberly Baer Design Associates, Inc. thrives inside a colorful, inviting nook in Venice, California. Enter and a dapper piglet wags hello. The fragrance of warm toast greets the nose, and then the magic of the place reveals itself.

Whatever you seek — from annual reports to logos, from websites to elaborate packaging solutions — is found here, created with a combination of deep thoughtfulness and inventive charm, sophisticated design and artful whimsy.

The players at KBDA have the knack of knowing how to marry the joy and exuberance of the seed vision with the nuts and bolts of pulling-it-off. With finesse, blatant elegance, and playfulness to boot, the collaborative spark of the firm meets all projects with an eye to unlocking its greatest communicative possibilities, while holding the client in hand. Human hand.

For Kimberly Baer Design Associates knows the ultimate purpose of the work is to talk to, whisper to, relate to...people.

They create the kind of information you want to touch: corporate identities without the crisis; annual reports that tell the story; packaging thàt won't leak, and websites that actually feel good.

1

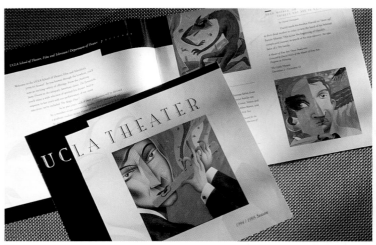

2

3

4

1. *Studio interior.*
2. *Theater subscription brochure.*
3. *Gourmet salsa packaging.*
4. *Gourmet spice packaging.*
5. *Annual report for communication
   software company.*

5

1

2

3

4

6

7

1. *Annual report for clinical testing company.*

2. *Annual report for manufacturer of voice mail equipment.*

3. *Catalog for lighting designer.*

4. *Annual report for healthcare company.*

5. *Logo for a rap music recording label.*

6. *Logo for company distributing products targeted to people in transition.*

7. *Logo for a cultural center in Los Angeles.*

8. *Annual report for a healthcare company.*

8

1

2

4

5

6

3

1. *Annual report for a company that develops toys based on licensed properties.*

2. *Annual report for a toy company.*

3. *Annual report for philanthropic foundation.*

4. *Logo for a gourmet, roasted chicken restaurant.*

5. *Logo for non profit organization.*

6. *Logo for a gourmet Tuscan restaurant.*

7. *Capabilities brochure for philanthropic organization.*

7

24

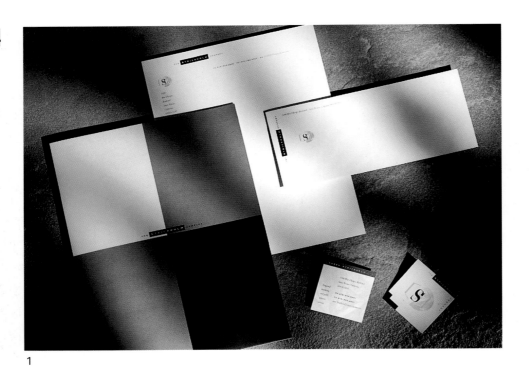

1

2

1. *Identity system for public relations firm.*

2. *Direct mail promotion for national food company.*

3. *Annual report for a manufacturer of computer networking devices.*

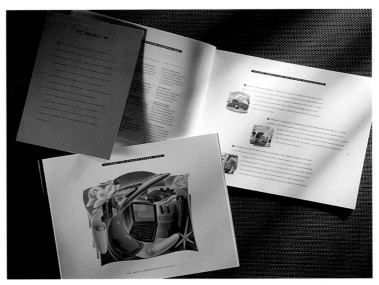

3

bielenberg
design

26

1

2

3

4

Bielenberg Design's philosophy is built upon the premise that the professional practice of graphic design is primarily about engineering a connection between a message and an audience. A cerebral, concept-driven approach underlies all work produced by the firm.

Founded in 1990 in San Francisco, California, a second office was opened in Boulder, Colorado in 1995. The firm's work has been chosen by The Library of Congress for its permanent Art & Design Collection in Washington, DC, the San Francisco Museum of Modern Art, and the "Good Design" collection at the Chicago Athenaeum.

In 1991, Bielenberg Design, under the pseudonym Virtual Telemetrix, Inc., began a continuing series of self-initiated and funded creative projects that address issues related to the practice of graphic design. Pieces in the series include: a poster, a book, an annual report, a catalog, and a t-shirt. Currently under development are a virtual design competition and a web site.

John Bielenberg believes that the Virtual Telemetrix series exposes inaccurate assumptions about graphic design. "Although graphic design is generally thought of as a creative profession, designers are sometimes victims of preset patterns of thinking that inhibit them from free creativity and from understanding the essential nature of what they do. Just like an addict creates a lust for drugs or alcohol, the designer can develop a craving for the new, the visually compelling and the beautiful. The image can become an end in itself and the message buried in subservience to the graphic language."

1. *John Bielenberg*
2. *Teri Vasarhelyi*
3. *Marion Radloff*
4. *Chuck Denison*
5-9. *Virtual Telemetrix 1993 Annual Report.*

5

6

7

8

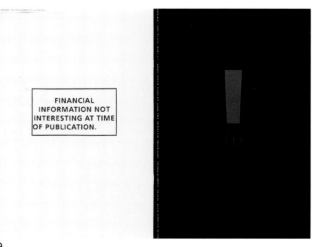

9

1-12. *Ceci n'est pas un catalogue (This is not a catalog) from Virtual Telemetrix.*

1

2

3

4

abcdefghijklm
nopqrstuvwxyz
ABCDEFGHIJ
KLMNOPQRS
TUVWXYZ
1234567890
(.,;:?!$&*){ÄÖ
ÜØÆŒÇ}

5

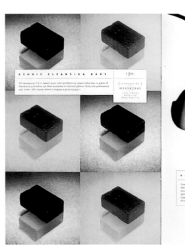

6

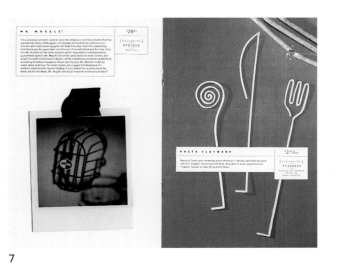

7

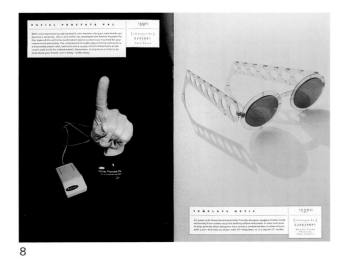

8

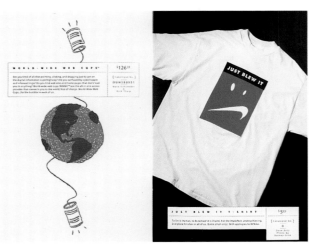

9

10

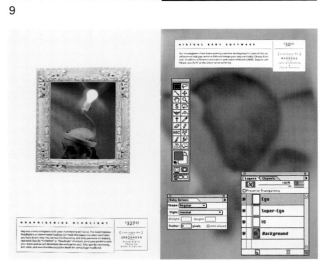

11

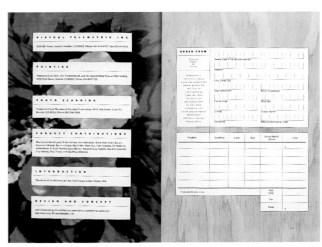

12

THIS IS THE 3RD IN A SERIES OF TEN.
IN THIS ISSUE JOHN BIELENBERG
SEARCHES FOR THE EXISTENCE
OF UTOPIA WHEN THE
FUTURE IS REDUCED TO THE
FOUR WALLS OF A PRISON CELL.
JOHN'S SUBJECT IS A WOMAN
AND A CONVICT,
INCARCERATED FOR LIFE.

UTOPIA IS A NEW COATED LINE FROM
APPLETON PAPERS. JOHN'S ISSUE IS
PRINTED ON UTOPIA TWO, BLUE WHITE
GLOSS, 80LB. TEXT

1

2

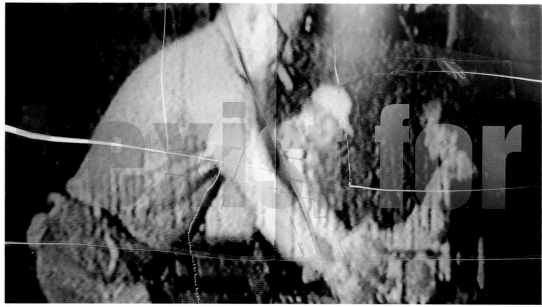

3

1-5. Brochure to promote Utopia, a new line of coated paper from Appleton Papers.

4

5

1-4. *Virtual Telemetrix Web Site. The Web is dead, long live the Web.*

32

1

2

3

4

blackdog

34 The BlackDog Philosophy:

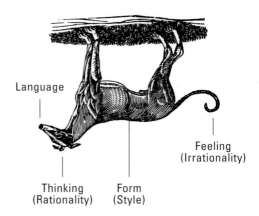

Language

Thinking
(Rationality)

Form
(Style)

Feeling
(Irrationality)

Photo: Will Mosgrove

Mark Fox graduated from UCLA with a degree in Fine Arts in 1984. His work is included in the Library of Congress permanent design collection, and the architecture and design collection of the San Francisco Museum of Modern Art.

Clients include Autodesk, Nike, Oracle, SFMOMA, and Warner Bros. Records. In addition, Mark has created logos for seven restaurants, including Embarko in San Francisco and The Buckeye Roadhouse in Mill Valley.

He has taught graphic design at the California College of Arts and Crafts, and is a past president of the San Francisco chapter of the American Institute of Graphic Arts. He has written for *Communication Arts,* and wrote the introduction to *The New American Logo,* published by Madison Square Press in 1994.

All work designed and illustrated by Mark Fox, unless otherwise noted.

*Cover design for a collection of poetry
titled* Where You Form the Letter L *by
Denise Liddell Lawson. Design: Mark
Fox and Denise Liddell Lawson;
photography: David Peterson; publisher:
San Francisco State University.*

One of three posters for the 1996 Mill Valley Film Festival. The word cinema is related to the term kinetic, which means movement— hence movie, motion picture. The design seeks to create a sense of movement through the juxtaposition of two photographs in a target formation. Design and photography: Mark Fox; agency: Scheyer/SF.

Silk screen poster announcing the California College of Arts and Crafts' annual Adopt-a-Book event. Text is from Paul Rand's essay "From Cassandre to Chaos."

Poster publicizing the Design Lecture Series sponsored by the San Francisco Museum of Modern Art. This particular series featured iconoclastic artists and designers such as Jenny Holzer, Tibor Kalman, and Vaughan Oliver. The eye and crossed hammers refers to the literal meaning of iconoclast: an "icon smasher."

1

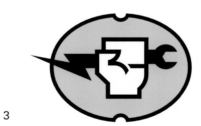

2

3

1. *Logo for Unity 2, an interracial two-member band. Art Direction: Mary Ann Dibs, Warner Bros. Records.*

2. *Logo for Red Herring, a retail store featuring one-of-a-kind housewares from around the world.*

3. *Logo for Webfactory, consultants specializing in network, Web site, and database management.*

4. *Logo for the Dallas Burn, a professional soccer team. Art Direction: Katy Tisch, NIKE.*

4

BLACKDOG ®
330 Sir Francis Drake Boulevard, Suite A, San Anselmo, CA 94960   415.258.9663   FAX 415.258.9681   E-MAIL BlackDogma@aol.com

Catalog cover for HarperCollins West. The design uses Imogen Cunningham's famous image of the west, Aloe, *to create a map of the publisher's territory. Art Direction: Michele Wetherbee and Shelly Meadows, HarperCollins.*

tom
bonauro
design

42 Tom Bonauro works as a graphic designer and art director. He founded his San Francisco design studio in 1979. His work emphasizes the abstraction of the objective world by employing alternating viewpoints and opening boundaries both in print and his film/video work. In the latter, the viewer is disoriented by the elimination of reference points and the sequencing of objects in motion in such a way as to frustrate his or her expectations of three-dimensional space.

His work transforms the urban narratives that lie embedded in the objects of everyday life into larger-than-life icons. Images often used in his work are not literally connected to any specific product. They can be irreverent, they are interesting in themselves, and they evoke a visceral response which enhances the "atmosphere" of any given piece.

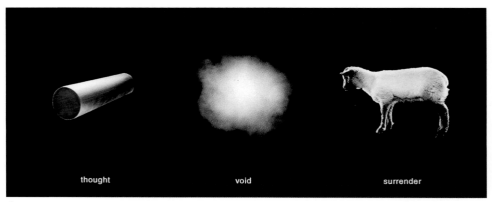

1

2

3

4

43

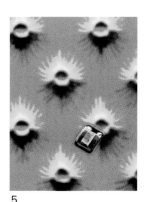

5

6

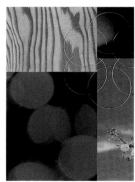

7

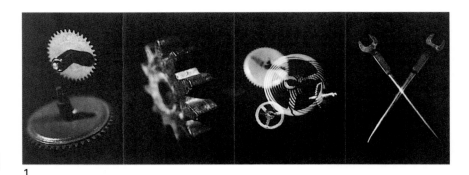

1

2

1-2. *Function Engineering mailer.*

3-5. *Spreads from self promo book.*

6-8. *Todd Oldham Fall 1996 Collection Invitation.*

9. *SCIARC Fall Lecture Series poster.*

10. *SCIARC Fall Lecture Series mailer.*

11. *Margaret Jenkins Dance Company announcement.*

6

7

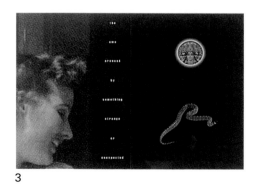

3

5

4

8

44

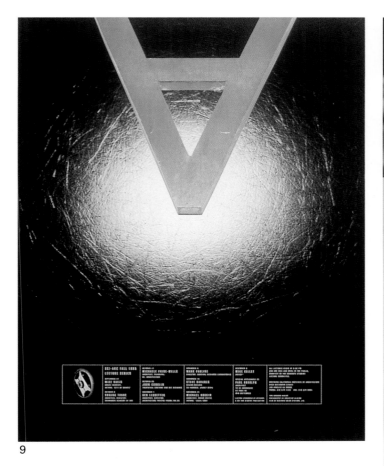

9

11

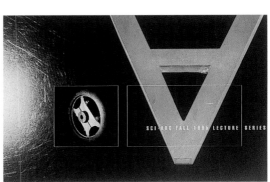

10

1

2

1-2. Yang Snowboard clothing catalog.

3-5. Levi's® 501® post cards.

6-7. Dork Films ID.

8. Levi's® 501® poster.

9-10. Levi's® 501® bus kings.

11. Levi's® 501® phone kiosk.

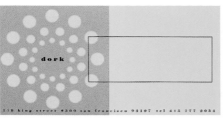

6

7

46

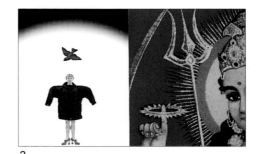

3

4

5

8

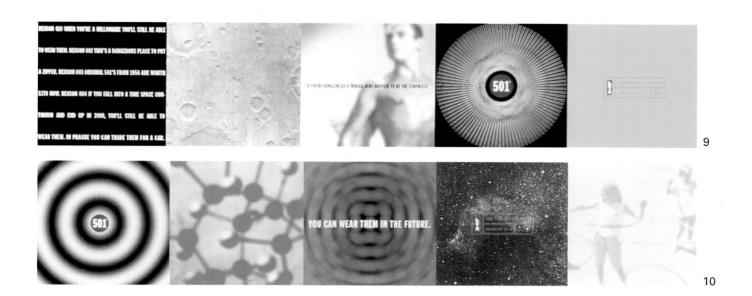

9

10

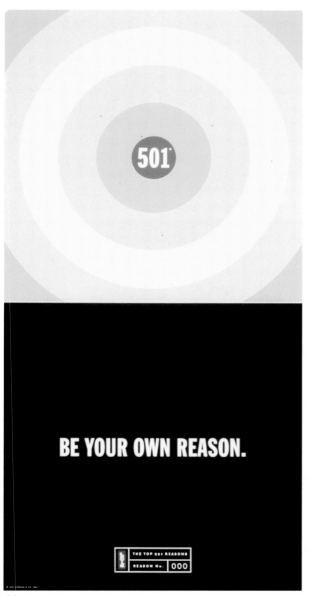

11

1-4. *Levi's® 501® posters.*

48

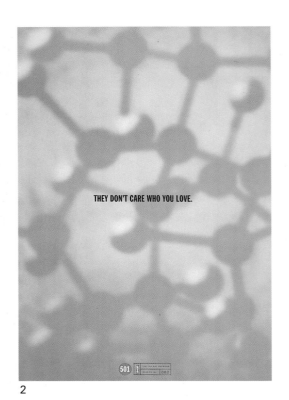

bright
strategic
design

LA

50

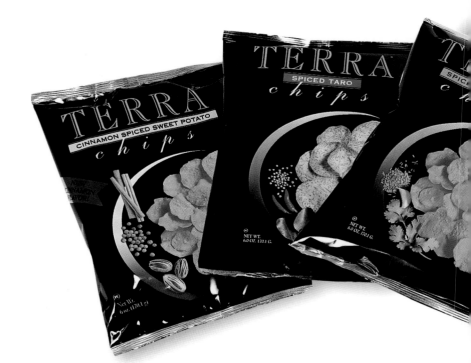

Bright's reputation is based on the development and implementation of corporate and product brand identities and dealing with their specific needs in the marketplace. Their approach is to target the wants and needs of the intended consumer and then produce appealing graphics that motivate the consumer to purchase. This proven methodology has been formed from years of working closely with clients who truly understand their marketing needs and subsequently translating those needs into successful design that is delivered on time and on budget.

Bright has been providing award winning strategic brand identity and packaging design for over 20 years. We have a complete understanding of product branding and positioning, as well as strategic design. Bright recognizes that a strong identity and packaging system is not only visually important for brand recognition and shelf appeal, but it must make sense from a business point of view as well. Bright has an established history in strategizing and creating package design projects, branding and sales support materials for key international brands. Through this process, we have developed an understanding of and familiarity with marketing objectives, design and production requirements. This ultimately has resulted in a depth of product and category knowledge that can be readily applied to new design projects for faster turnaround time and targeted, sales oriented graphic design.

1. *Terra Chips: Exciting, sophisticated packaging for an exotic snack made from vegetable roots. This award winning design complements the naturally colorful chips.*

2. *Langer: A fresh, new identity and complete redesign for Langer's main fruit juice line that includes a variety of sizes in 18 flavors.*

1

52

1. *Allergan Complete: A global identity and branded packaging program for Allergan contact lens care division, including naming.*

2. *Allergan Azelex: This new skin product was named and packaged to reach people with severe acne problems.*

3. *World Cup 1994: This signature collateral piece was designed to generate corporate sales for World Cup.*

4. *Veggibles: Designed original packaging for an all natural food product.*

5. *Kirin: Both Kirin Draft Beer and Kirin Light Beer were redesigned and repositioned to appeal to a larger market.*

6. *Ortho: Identity and packaging for Ortho.*

1

2

6

3

4

5

MILLER BEER

Facing increased competition,
Miller Brewing decided to
reposition their top four brands;
Miller Lite and Lite Ice, Miller
Genuine Draft and Miller Genuine
Draft Light. Bright was selected
to redesign these top brands.

All of these brands reflect
the use of a new crest to build a
stronger Miller identity.
Bright was responsible for
designing all the primary and
secondary packaging.
Sales are up.

New Los Angeles Partnership symbol represents the diversity of cultures, the mountains, the sea and the sun that unites over 27 cities in Southern California. The "we" symbol was used in commercials and advertisements promoting Los Angeles as the place to be.

1. Mandalay Entertainment, a film production company.

2. Game Show Network, a new cable channel with over 20,000 game shows.

3. Gratis, a Beverly Hills restaurant offering fat free cuisine.

4. NATPE, National Association of Television Program Executives-representing local TV and cable channels.

5. California Community Foundation, a non-profit foundation which grants awards for community needs.

6. Los Angeles Convention and Visitors Bureau

7. CETRA, China external trade association. A global company representing Taiwan.

8. Mercury Marine, manufacturer of wave crafts.

1

2

Together we're the best. Los Angeles.

3

4

5

6

7

8

curtis
design

58

Curtis Design was created in 1989 by two brothers, David and Brad Curtis.....and after seven years in business, they have grown to complement each other quite well. Brad is more outgoing, so he handles sales and marketing while Dave maintains the creative vision behind design and production. "In a way", says Dave, "I make certain the work is creative, Brad makes sure it's effective."

Their two objectives share a common emphasis—creating an environment that encourages designers to test themselves within the parameters of the design problem. "We want our solutions to make an impact in their respective industries—and that means continually investing our designers with the education, equipment and inspiration they need to succeed creatively."

Apparently this collaborative focus works. With an impressive client list ranging from Ghirardelli Chocolate and The Stroh Brewery to 3Com and Intel, Curtis Design has created identity programs, packaging systems and retail environments for "everything from chocolate chips to computer chips," jokes Brad.

1

1. *Curtis Design Studio and staff.*

3

2

2-3. *Poster, invite and reply card utilize a clever metaphor for the San Francisco Museum of Modern Art; The Modern Ball "Hollywood Hats."*

1

2

60

3

4

1. *Identity for Caravali Coffee Company.*

2. *Identity and package design for Nibbler Farms.*

3. *Ghirardelli's Cocolat design targets the mass merchandising class of trade.*

4. *Ghirardelli Classico— a special occasion gift item.*

5. *Ghirardelli's upscale signature line.*

6-7. *Identity and packaging system for the world's largest producer of garlic products.*

8. *Leinenkugel's packaging system created for Miller Brewing Co.*

9. *Packaging highlights expandability and consistent branding of The Stroh Brewery, Augsburger Beer.*

5

6

7

8

9

1

2

1. *Informational brochure created for Affymetrix's Genechip analysis system.*

2. *Identity and package design for Norian's Skeletal Repair System.*

3. *The AIGA San Francisco Fiscal Fitness Four direct mail piece.*

3

4

5

6

7

8

4. *Identity developed for Pen-based software owned by Microsoft.*

5. *Logotype for the Coca-Cola Company, Glacial Mist Beverages.*

6. *"Network-in-a-box" solution for 3Com Corporation emphasizing easy installation.*

7. *Poster design for Marin Shakespeare Company.*

8. *CD, manual and brochure design system created for 3Com Corporation.*

1

2

64

3

4

5

1. *Ravioli's identity and mascot for Italian fast food retailer.*

2. *Javalanche instant iced latte packaging for Caravali Coffee Company.*

3. *Packaging system for Granny Goose Foods' Kettle Chips product line.*

4. *Thai Kitchen packaging system developed for Epicurean International.*

5. *Nature's Burger highlights taste appeal.*

evenson
design
group

LA

What's your philosophy?

Look. Listen. Acknowledge that you don't know it all and never will — but take the time or make the time to learn more. And to the extent that you can, work for people who cultivate a similar philosophy.

What do you listen to? To your inner voice? To what your clients say?

Both — but we put our inner voice at the service of meeting the client's needs. We're not fine artists. We'll have plenty of chances to hit that edge, but the point of it all is commercial reproduction, not self-indulgence.

How is the role of the designer changing?

Designers need to be more technically proficient than ever. Clients are becoming more knowledgeable, and many now have extensive in-house capabilities. We enjoy the full range of team relationships — our greatest value has always been in providing fresh insights and helping clients to "step outside the box." In that respect, our role remains the same.

And what about clients, anyway?

Seek their input, acknowledge their thoughts, and make sure they enjoy the process.

1. Stan Evenson, illustrated by his son Peter (age 6).

2. Evenson Design Group holiday promotion.

3. Evenson Design Group summer promotion.

66

1

2

3

2

3

1. Logo for International CPA firm
Gelfand, Rennert, Feldman & Brown

2. Wedding invitation.

3. Capabilities brochure for Johnson
& Higgins, a risk management
insurance company.

4. Promotional package for
Anderson Printing.

4

Kingpin

1

2

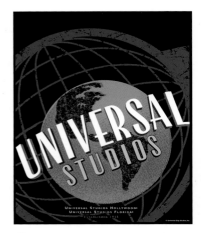

3

4

5

6

1. Logo for the feature film Kingpin.

2. Signage design for Disneyland's The Coffee House.

3. Shopping bag design for Universal Studios.

4. Promotional material for The Disney Channel Home Satellite Services.

5. Universal Studios Jurassic Outfitters' store shopping bag.

6. Proposed logo design for DreamWorks' Toys.

1. Logo for Warner Bros. new Sports Licensing Division.

2. Proposed logo for a computer company.

3. Proposed symbol for Matria Health Care.

4. Proposed logo for Americast, a telecommunications company.

5. Logo design for NFL team, The New England Patriots.

6. Symbol for CoLab, a creative development team.

7. Logo for Thums Long Beach Company.

8. Proposed logo for a telecommunications company.

1

2

3

4

5

6

7

8

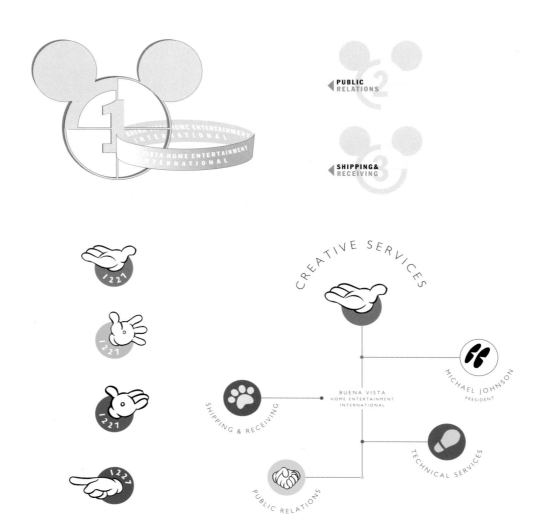

PUBLIC
RELATIONS

SHIPPING&
RECEIVING

CREATIVE SERVICES

MICHAEL JOHNSON
PRESIDENT

BUENA VISTA
HOME ENTERTAINMENT
INTERNATIONAL

SHIPPING & RECEIVING

TECHNICAL SERVICES

PUBLIC RELATIONS

1

1. Interior signage identification
system for Buena Vista Home
Entertainment International.

2. Direct mailer for The Disney
Channel.

2

1

2

3

4

5

1. Logo for The Farm Store Restaurant.

2. Product line packaging for DayRunner Personal and Professional Organizers.

3. Packaging for Disneyland's The Coffee House.

4. Proposed packaging for Bold Detergent.

5. Proposed logo for Mountain Dew, a PepsiCola Company.

4445 Overland Avenue Culver City, California 90230 310.204.1995 fax 310.204.4879

1

© Paul Spinelli/NFLP

2

1. Logo for 1994 World Soccer Games.

2. Logo, uniform and helmet design for NFL team, The New England Patriots.

3. Logo and apparel application for Warner Bros. new Sports Licensing Division.

3

hunt
design
associates

LA

Formerly known as Wayne Hunt Design, the firm has emerged as a creative force in the quickly evolving field of environmental graphic design. "We merge the creative sequences of graphic design with the technology and phasing of architecture." says company principal Wayne Hunt.

Founded in 1977, the Pasadena-based firm develops signage and graphics programs for entertainment environments, retail spaces, public buildings, cities and parks. The practice is geared for large scale projects such as theme parks, airports and museums.

"We also go a long way to do our work." says Hunt, noting the company has worked recently in Japan, Korea, Mexico, England and Germany, not to mention 11 states in the USA.

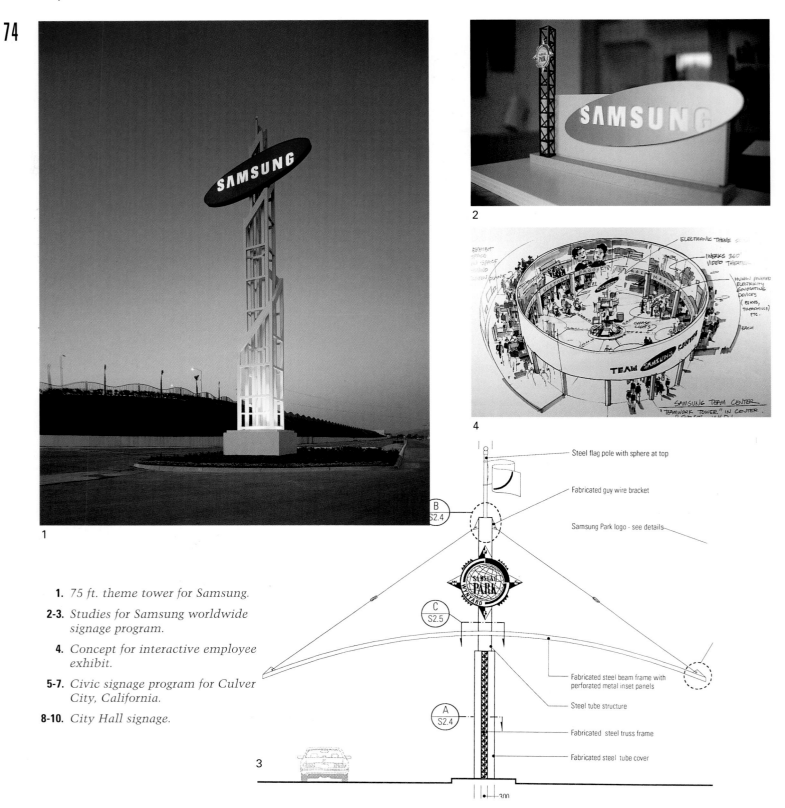

1

2

4

Steel flag pole with sphere at top

Fabricated guy wire bracket

Samsung Park logo - see details

Fabricated steel beam frame with perforated metal inset panels

Steel tube structure

Fabricated steel truss frame

Fabricated steel tube cover

3

1. *75 ft. theme tower for Samsung.*

2-3. *Studies for Samsung worldwide signage program.*

4. *Concept for interactive employee exhibit.*

5-7. *Civic signage program for Culver City, California.*

8-10. *City Hall signage.*

5

6

8

7

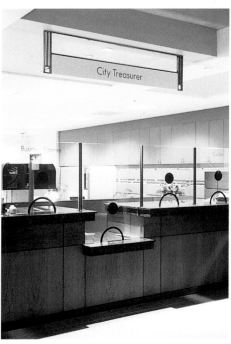

10

9

1

4

2

3

5

6

7

10

11

12

13

8

1-3. *World Cup USA '94 signage.*

4-5. *Lake Elsinore Diamond signage.*

6-8. *Children's exhibit at Los Angeles Zoo.*

9-13. *Environmental graphics at New Jersey State Aquarium*

1

2

4

5

3

1-5. *Graphics for shows and attractions at Porto Europa in Japan.*

6. *Logo for a music festival.*

7. *Logo for a German theme park.*

8. *Logo for a sports district.*

9-10. *Signage concepts for McCarran International Airport, Las Vegas.*

Festival Santa Anita®1994

6

MUSICA · COMIDA · ARTE

SPACE
PARK
BREMEN

7

SPORTSTOWN
ANAHEIM

8

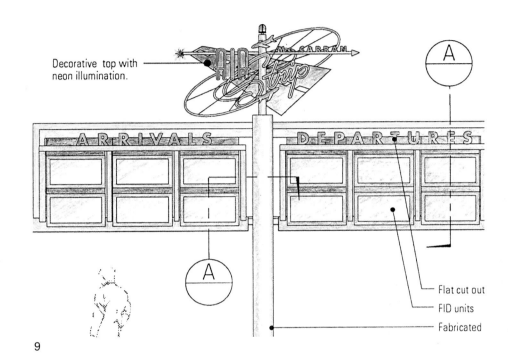

Decorative top with
neon illumination.

Ⓐ

Ⓐ

Flat cut out

FID units

Fabricated

9

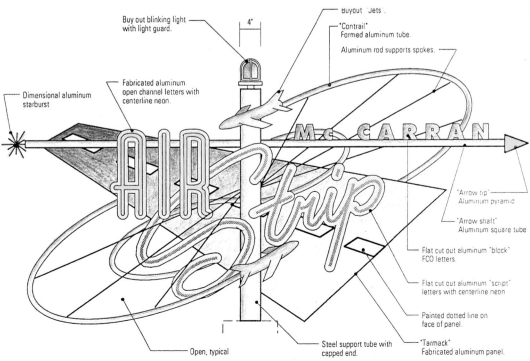

Buy out blinking light
with light guard.

4"

Buyout "Jets".

"Contrail"
Formed aluminum tube.

Aluminum rod supports spokes.

Fabricated aluminum
open channel letters with
centerline neon.

Dimensional aluminum
starburst

"Arrow tip"
Aluminum pyramid

"Arrow shaft"
Aluminum square tube

Flat cut out aluminum "block"
FCO letters.

Flat cut out aluminum "script"
letters with centerline neon

Painted dotted line on
face of panel.

Open, typical

Steel support tube with
capped end.

"Tarmack"
Fabricated aluminum panel.

10

HUNT DESIGN ASSOCIATES
87 North Raymond Avenue, Suite 215, Pasadena, CA 91103   818.793.7847   Fax: 818.793.2549

80

1

2

3

1-3. *Graphics program for a shopping district, Pasadena, California.*

SF

ingalls
+
associates

82 After seven years working for museums, magazines, record & film companies, restaurants and various corporations in Los Angeles, Tom Ingalls was lured to San Francisco to work for *Rolling Stone.* In 1978 the magazine moved to New York, but Tom stayed in San Francisco and formed Ingalls + Associates to focus on his first love, book design.

Since then, his studio has designed over 100 complete books and 700 book jackets. His love for cooking led to many cookbook projects and subsequently food and wine packaging. The Bay Area also produced clients that needed online design and support materials for the computer industry.

Looking around his studio you can spot designs for cigar and wine labels, restaurants signs and menus, home pages and business cards for information companies, a graphic standards manual and even a logo for a golf group.

Their current projects include a book/video for a worldwide travel service, a new French/Japanese restaurant, Italian wine packaging and a monthly magazine for Hong Kong, Tokyo and Seoul.

Tom believes that effective design should urge the viewer (prospect) to sight your product, lock-up, and become engaged by its sense of purpose. This approach of integrating form and function with a pleasing visual experience adds value to the content of the piece. Tom feels design should be the crystal goblet that illuminates the perfect clarity of the wine.

1. *Zip case & disk*
Client: Ingalls + Associates
Art Director: Tom Ingalls
Designer: Caroline Byrne

2. *Uncle John's Band logo*
Client: Herb Greene
Art Director: Tom Ingalls
Designer: Caryl Gorska

3. *Dead Days*
Client: Stacy Quinn
Art Director: Herb Greene
Designer: Tom Ingalls
Photographer: Herb Greene
Author: Herb Greene
Publisher: Acid Test Productions

1

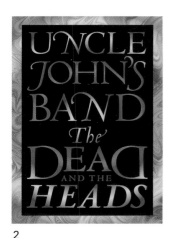

2

4

4. *Antiseptic Surgery*
Client: Ursus Books
Art Director: Tom Ingalls
Designer: Tom Ingalls
Author: Joseph Lister
Publisher: Ursus Books

5. *New Architecture San Francisco*
Client: Chronicle Books
Art Director: Tom Ingalls
Designer: Tom Ingalls
Photographer: Christopher Irion
Author: James Shay
Publisher: Chronicle Books

6. *The Tao of Natural Breathing*
Client: Dennis Lewis
Art Director: Tom Ingalls
Designers: Tom Ingalls and Caroline Byrne
Author: Dennis Lewis
Publisher: Mountain Wind Publishing

5

3

6

84

2

1. *Hellish Relish*
   Client: Harper Collins
   Art Director: Tom Ingalls
   Designer: Tom Ingalls
   Photographer: Eduardo Fuss
   Author: Sharon N. Niederman
   Publisher: Harper Collins

2. *The American and Asian Grill*
   Client: Chronicle Books
   Art Directors: Tom Ingalls and David Barish
   Designers: Tom Ingalls and Tracy Dean
   Photographer: Dennis Bettencout
   Authors: Tom Ingalls and David Barish
   Publisher: Chronicle Books
   Food Styling: Erés

3. *Dinner By Design*
   Client: Jane Dunne
   Art Director: Tom Ingalls
   Designer: Tom Ingalls
   Illustrator: Rebekah Lee
   Publisher: American Center for Design

4. *Restaurant logo*
   Client: David Cohn
   Art Director: Tom Ingalls
   Designer: Tom Ingalls

5. *Brandy logo*
   Client: Alambic, Inc.
   Art Director: Tom Ingalls
   Designer: Tom Ingalls

1

3

ATRIUM

4

GERMAIN-ROBIN

5

6

7

8

6. *Stratford Wines*
Client: Richard Paleski
Art Director: Tom Ingalls
Designer: Harumi Kubo
Illustrator: Harumi Kubo

7. *Ziretta*
Client: Richard Paleski
Art Director: Tom Ingalls
Designer: Caroline Byrne

8. *VillaRica*
Client: Richard Paleski
Art Director: Tom Ingalls
Designer: Caroline Byrne
Ilustrator: Caroline Byrne

86

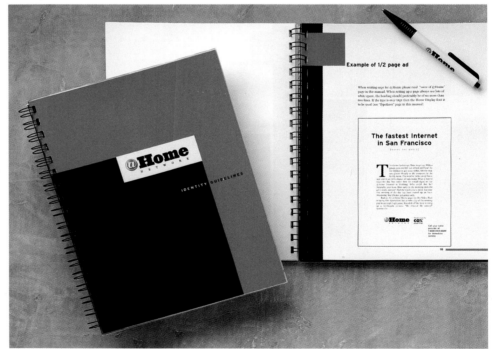

4

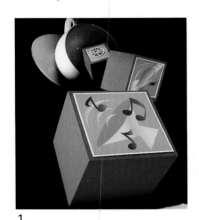

1

1. *Hot Java*
   Client: Margaret Rowlands
   Art Director: Tom Ingalls
   Designer: Caryl Gorska
   Photographer: Mark Yohan
   Publisher: Sybex Computer Books

2. *Windows 95*
   Client: Margaret Rowlands
   Art Director: Tom Ingalls
   Designer: Caryl Gorska
   Illustrator: Caryl Gorska
   Photographer: Mark Yohan
   Publisher: Sybex Computer Books

3. *Access the Internet*
   Client: Margaret Rowlands
   Art Director: Tom Ingalls
   Designer: Caryl Gorska
   Illustrator: Rebekah Lee
   Publisher: Sybex Computer Books

4. *Various*
   Client: Margaret Rowlands
   Art Director: Tom Ingalls
   Designer: Tom Ingalls
   Photographer: Mark Yohan
   Publisher: Sybex Computer Books

5. *Identity Guidelines*
   Client: @Home
   Art Director: Roger Black
   Designers: Tom Ingalls and
   Tania Leach
   Publisher: @Home

5

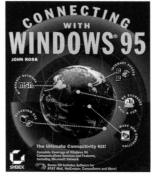

2

3

6

6. Home page
Client: Peter Karnig
Art Director: Tom Ingalls
Designer: Tania Leach
Publisher: Infomatix

7. Travel service logo
Client: World Wide Travel
Art Director: Tom Ingalls
Designer: Tania Leach

8. Business identity
Client: Body Adventure
Art Director: Tom Ingalls
Designer: Margot Scaccabarrozzi
Illustrator: Margot Scaccabarrozzi

9. Beauty products packaging
Client: The Body Adventure
Art Director: Tom Ingalls
Designer: Caroline Byrne

7

8

9

I N G A L L S   +   A S S O C I A T E S

Ingalls + Associates 10 Arkansas Street, San FranciscoCalifornia 94107   Tel: 415.626.6395 Fax: 415.626.6395 email: ingalls@sirius.com

3

88

The City

2

1

1-2. *Cigar label, matches*
Client: Fumé
Art Director: Tom Ingalls
Designers: Caryl Gorska and
Tom Ingalls
Illustrator: Caryl Gorska

3. *Food label*
Client: Village Orchard
Art Director: Tom Ingalls
Designer: Harumi Kubo
Illustrator: Harumi Kubo

4. *Japanese magazine*
Client: Greg Vass
Art Director: Tom Ingalls
Designer: Caroline Byrne

4

lisa
levin
design

90 Lisa Levin Design is an award-winning San Francisco Bay Area graphic design firm that creates corporate identity programs, annual reports, collateral and packaging for corporations and non-profit organizations.

As proponents of intelligent design, they strive to find creative solutions that are grounded in a thorough understanding of their clients' needs.

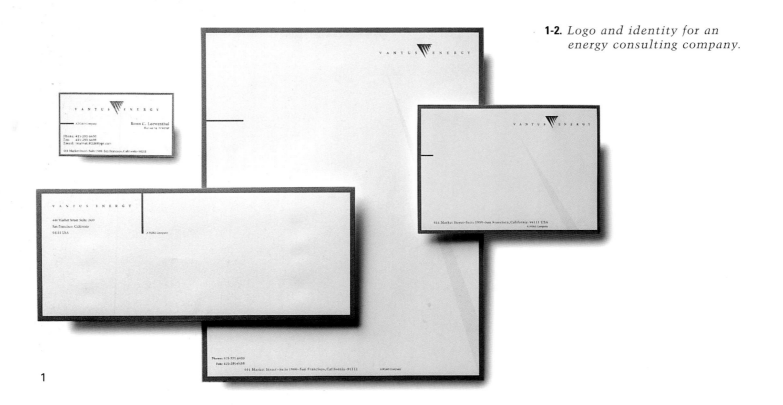

1-2. *Logo and identity for an energy consulting company.*

1

2

VANTUS ENERGY

3

4

3. *A tabloid-sized journal filled with news and information for Saturn car-owners.*

4. *Proposed logo for Vantus Energy.*

5. *Eye-catching fundraising materials for Public Television.*

6. *By combining poetic images with one- and two-color printing on three different paper stocks, this produced award winning annual report was produced within the tight budget of this non-profit company.*

5

6

1

1-2. *Annual and quarterly reports for a software company.*

2

3

4

5

3-4. *Two books designed and produced for Chronicle Books.*

5. *Logo for a restaurant that serves California/Asian cuisine.*

6. *Media kit for The Sierra Club's* SIERRA MAGAZINE.

3

1

2

3

4

1. *Mail order catalogs for The Nature Company designed to reflect the store interiors.*

2-4. *Logo, identity system and video packaging for a children's video production company called Firedog Pictures.*

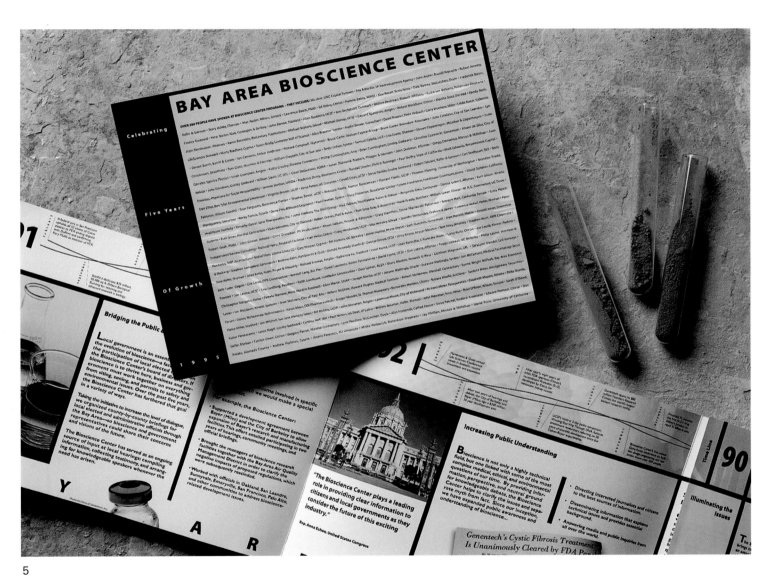

5

5. *Annual report for a non-profit agency that provides the SF Bay Area with information on biotechnology.*

96

1

scott
morgan

1. *By using a sheer vellum envelope,*
this logo and stationery system
showcases the photographer's
colorful and surrealistic images.

louey/rubino
design
group

LA

98 Louey/Rubino Design Group's philosophy is quite simple: They believe design without a defined message is merely decoration. They specialize in communication; clear, precise concepts that get to the point and cut through the clutter. Bold simple messages that speak to the audience; always set in a visually dynamic and appropriate stage. "The symbiotic union of language and visual form is what defines communications," states Robert Louey, Partner and Creative Director of the Santa Monica-based firm with an office in New York and an affiliate sister company in Jakarta, Indonesia.

Founded in 1984 by Robert Louey and Regina Rubino, Louey/Rubino Design Group Inc. is a full-service marketing communications firm specializing in corporate communications, strategic marketing, and related promotional and advertising programs.

The company has served many leading corporations, on an international scale, for over 13 years, including Coopers & Lybrand, The Hero Group, Kaufman and Broad, Lexus Financial Services, Mandarin Oriental, MGM-Pathe Communications Co., PacifiCare Health Systems, Rockwell, and Tri Polyta Indonesia.

Louey/Rubino Design Group's work is included in the Library of Congress Permanent Collection and has appeared in The Mead Show, AR100, Print, How, Graphis, Communication Arts, AIGA, The Type Directors Club and Interiors Magazine.

1

1. *Robert Louey and Regina Rubino*

2-4. *Self-promotion for their affiliate sister company in Jakarta, Indonesia*

2

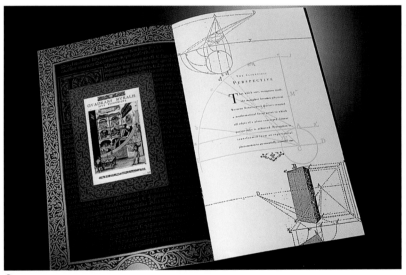

3

4

1-3. *Kaufman & Broad Home Corporation
1995 Annual Report.*
 4. *Lexus Financial Services marketing
brochure.*
 5. *Rockwell "Global Positioning
Systems" product brochure.*
6-7. *Reliance Steel & Aluminum Co. 1995
Annual Report.*
8-9. *PacifiCare Health Systems 1995
Annual Report.*

100

1

2

3

3

4

5

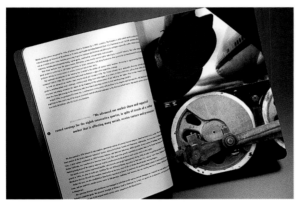

6

8

7

9

1-5. *Series of promotional calendars in conjunction with Lithographix, Butler Paper Company, Hopper, Mead and Potlach.*

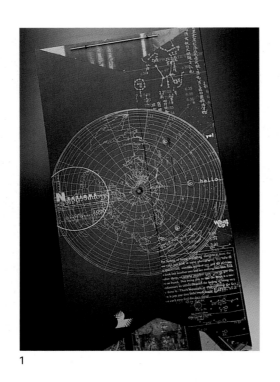

1

2

3

4

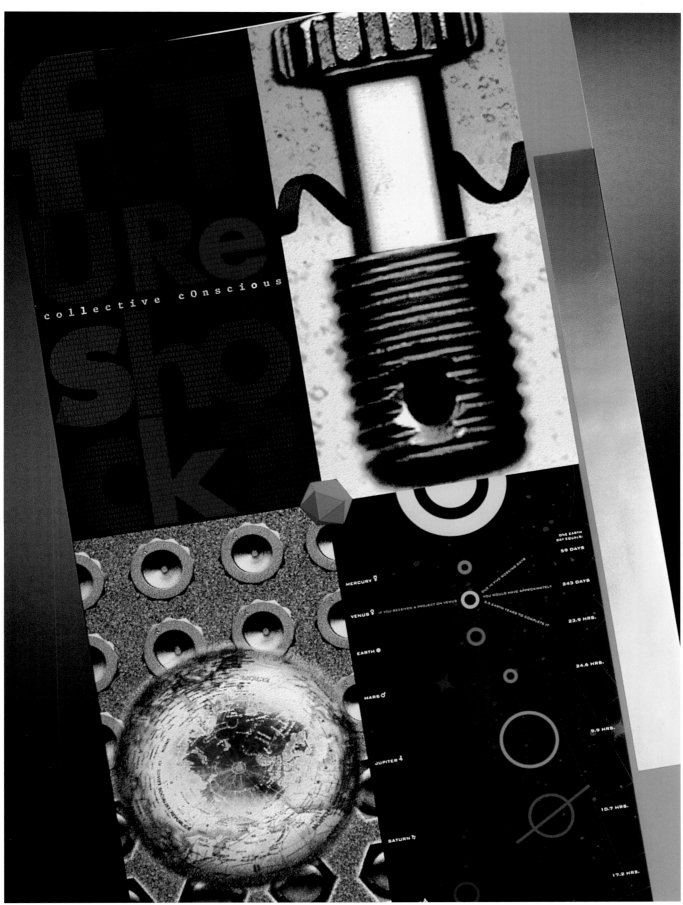

future shock

collective cOnscious

ONE EARTH
DAY EQUALS:

59 DAYS

MERCURY ☿

DUE IN FIVE WORKING DAYS

243 DAYS

VENUS ♀ IF YOU RECEIVED A PROJECT ON VENUS

YOU WOULD HAVE APPROXIMATELY

23.9 HRS.

2.3 EARTH YEARS TO COMPLETE IT

EARTH ⊕

24.6 HRS.

MARS ♂

9.9 HRS.

JUPITER ♃

10.7 HRS.

SATURN ♄

17.2 HRS.

LOUEY / RUBINO DESIGN GROUP INC.

2525 Main Street, Santa Monica, CA 90405   310.396.7724 FAX 310.396.1686
215 Park Avenue South, New York, NY 10003 212.777.4220 FAX 212.777.4261

104

1

3

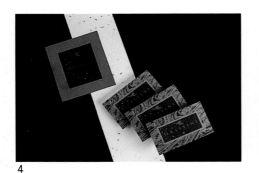

4

5

6

7

8

9

1-3. *Identity system for Le Bar Bat Niteclub in Hong Kong.*

4. *Identity for Grissini Italian restaurant.*

5. *Idenity for Zigolini Italian restaurant in Mandarin Oriental Jakarta.*

6. *Wedding invitation.*

7-8. *Identity for Zen Palate Restaurant in New York.*

9. *Promotion for Hopper Paper Company.*

luxon carrà

106

1

Luxon Carrà applies their strategic approach to a variety of design disciplines to help their clients communicate more effectively.

Their offices in San Francisco and London are headed by principals with global experience and an international perspective. Luxon Carrà's experience and design disciplines are sought by leaders in advanced technology, travel and leisure, petroleum, retail, communications and consulting.

While their projects are varied, a sound strategy and an insistence on creative excellence are at the heart of every solution. The people at Luxon Carrà are committed to using the power of design and communication to evoke a positive emotional response for their clients' products, brands and services. Enthusiasm for creative solutions that deliver results is apparent in all of their work.

2

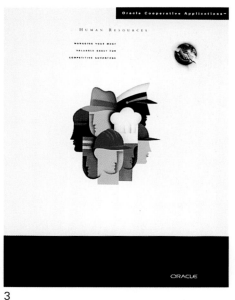

3

1. *Luxon Carrà, San Francisco CA.*

2. *Trade show identity for DataBlade® Technology, a division of Informix®.*

3. *Human Resources Applications brochure for Oracle®.*

4-5. *Standards and collateral for the SunSoft® brand use a unique visual vocabulary that works within Sun Microsystem's® graphic system.*

4

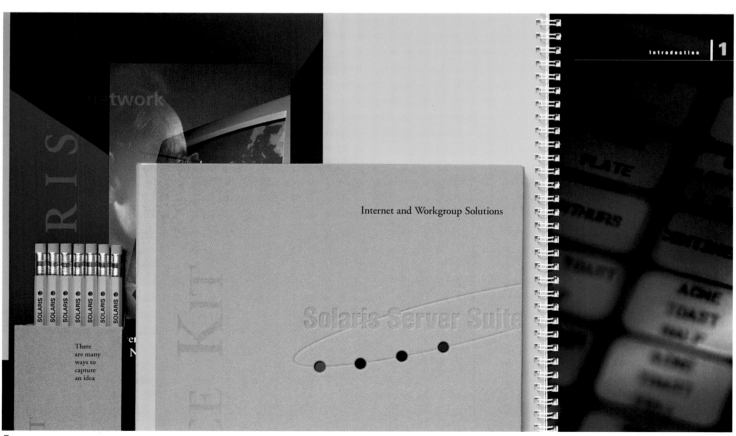

5

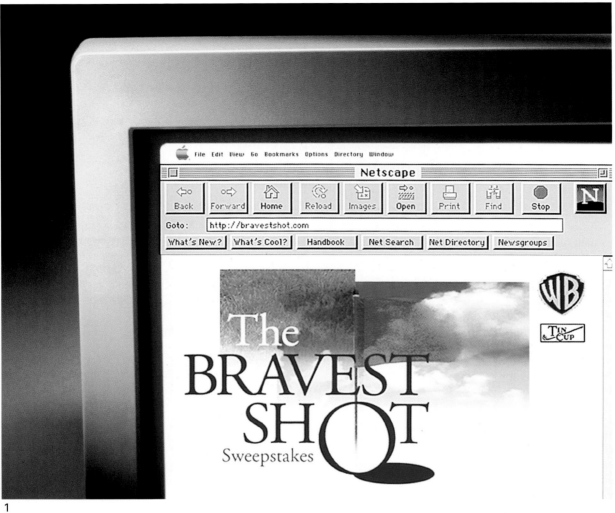

1

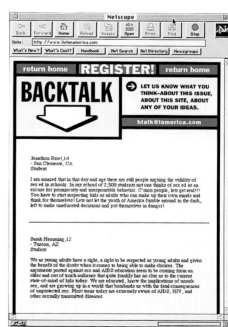

2

1-2. Web sites for a Warner Bros.® film and a national magazine have interactive features that encourage browser involvement.

3. Selections from an extensive collateral system which supports the Royal Cruise Line positioning of "luxury in a casual atmosphere."

Imagine a place where sea and sky meet. Where the sky is a blue you've seen only in dreams, and the sea is so clear it reflects each drift of the clouds. One by one, your senses awaken to adventure. Here, beyond the horizon, your odyssey begins.

Discover an Odyssey

of endless sea and sky

The Newsletter of Odyssey Club Members

odyssey club traveler

When you have the heart of a traveler, these are the sights you owe yourself: the African veldt at daybreak, the Taj Mahal in moonlight, the ancient capital of Vietnam and the enchanting smiles of Thai children. As 1996 draws near, Royal Cruise Line invites you to sail to the most exotic corners of the earth.

Fall 1995
Vol. 3 Issue 2

♛ Royal Cruise Line

Royal Cruise Line

Spa at Sea

For one glorious week, the world's most intimate and luxurious ship will become the world's most exclusive spa resort.

YOUR SHIPBOARD

Royal Cruise Line

Star Odyssey

Mighty Zeus, ruler of the sky all brazen with stars.

Stateroom Meal Menu

Welcome Aboard

And what a ship that takes you there, to vast horizons of flawless sky and brimming sea.

stanbu
Honolu
Colombo
ong B
Kota

Royal Cruise Lin

1 9 9 6

World Odyssey

Imagine seeing the world—from the

Royal Cruise Line

1996 World Odyssey
Shore Excursions

110

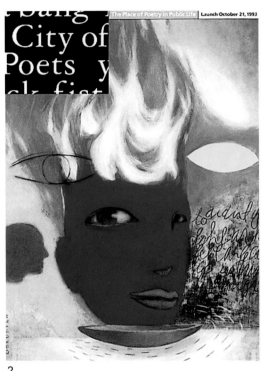

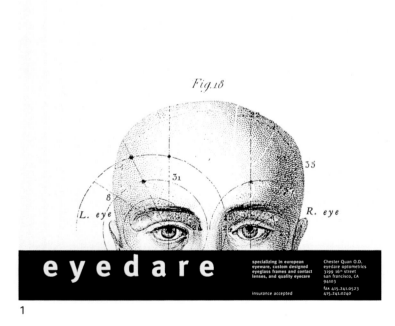

2

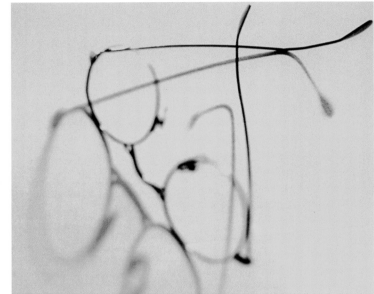

1

3

5

4

1. *Poster for Eyedare, a high-fashion eyeglass retailer.*

2. *Poster for the campaign for* City of Poets, *a San Francisco celebration of the written and spoken word.*

3. *One in a series of ads for the Sol y Luna® line of furniture.*

4. *New identity for Natural Wonders®, a national retailer.*

5. *New identity for the American Musical Theater of San Jose.*

1. *Employee guidelines for Pacific Telesis®.*

2. *Binder system for the Channel Program, one in a series of sales tools for Apple Computer®.*

112

1

2

SF

mauk
design

114 Mitchell Mauk is the Principal of Mauk Design, a firm based in San Francisco, specializing in exhibit design and corporate communications for technologically-oriented companies. The firm was formed ten years ago and puts special emphasis on the marketing integration of two and three dimensional images.

Recently Mauk Design completed a comprehensive corporate trade show program for Apple Computers, recycling some $5 million worth of parts. This project resulted in reduced set-up times, lowered shipping and drayage costs, and reinforcement of the Apple image.

Mauk Design's clients include Volkswagen of North America, Oral B, Trimble Navigation, Sun Microsystems, Microsoft, Disney, Pixar, Oracle, JavaSoft and Charles Schwab.

Mauk has won gold and silver awards from the IDSA and SEGD and was named "Exhibit Designer of the Year" in 1987. He was the first American designer to have a light design manufactured by the prestigious Italian lighting firm Artemide. His work has been featured in Communication Arts magazine, Print, Society of Typographic Arts, and Graphis, and is in the Permanent Collection of the Library of Congress.

1

Bancroft
Whitney

3

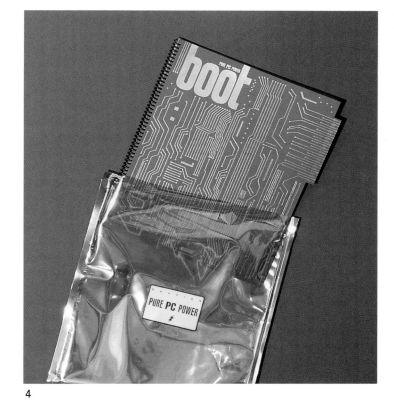

4

1. CD-ROM box for a Bancroft Whitneys' Law Desk law research programs.

2. Corporate identity for Bancroft Whitney, law publishers since 1886.

3. Interactive nametag for NetObjects Fusion rollout party. Attendees received a blank steel disk on a neckchain, then collected their name and magnetic buttons from various areas at the party.

4-5. Media kit for Boot magazine, a cutting edge publication emphasizing the home computer user.

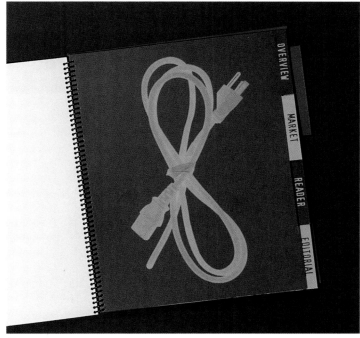

5

1

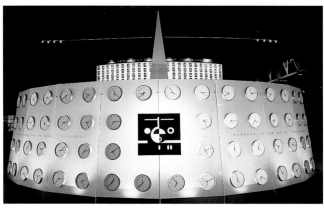

2

1-3. *A 30' x 40' trade show exhibit program for Duncan Aviation, a maintenance specialist for business jets. The exhibit utilizes high quality materials to illustrate Duncan's absolute reverence towards aircraft service. The photo wall of Duncan's employees emphasizes the importance of the individual.*

3

118

1

1. *The white appearance of the exhibit refers to Apple's historical graphic look. The pearl white color stands out from competitors on the trade show floor.*

2. *The X-shaped floorplan provides spacious aisles and passageways as well as easy access to demonstrations.*

3. *"Spider Displays" get powerbooks off desktop and put screens at eye level.*

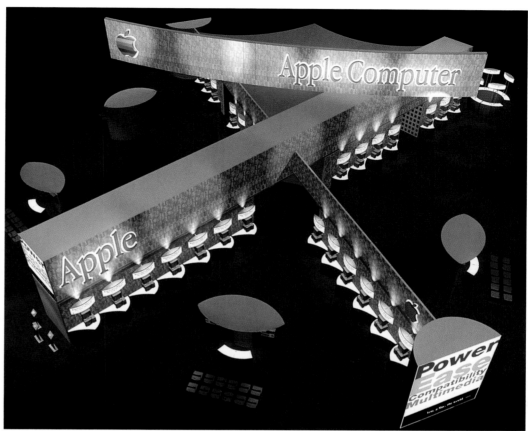

2

3

120

1

2

3

1-3. *Rollout event for Microsoft Internet Explorer 3.0. Glowing towers used stock scaffolding covered with flameproof theatrical paper.*

norman moore
design/art, inc.

LA

122 Born in Dundee, Scotland, Norman Moore studied Graphic Design at Harrow School of Art, London. He worked in London for two years at Ken Garland Associates and Ivor Kamlish Associates. He came to Los Angeles where he worked two years for Rod Dyer Inc. He returned to London to open his own design studio and after three years moved back to California as Art Director at MCA Records, Los Angeles until he established DesignArt, Inc.

His work includes packaging, magazines, corporate identities, annual reports, posters, book jackets and album covers. His work has received numerous awards and has been published by The Art Directors Club of Los Angeles, The New York Art Directors Club, The American Institute of Graphic Arts, The Type Directors Club, The Advertising Club of New York, The Western Art Directors Club, American Corporate Identity, The Designers and Art Directors Association/London, Graphis, and various design books and magazines.

1

2

3

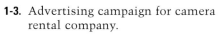

1-3. Advertising campaign for camera rental company.

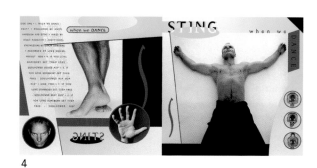

4

5

7

6

4. *CD single package.*

5. *CD single package.*

6. *Catalog cover.*

7. *Poster promoting album.*

124

1

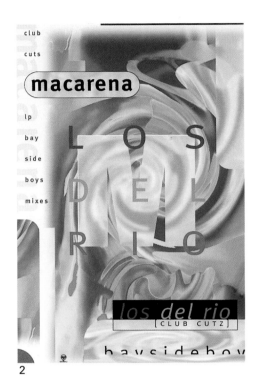

2

4

3

5

6

1. *Poster for film music company.*

2. *Poster for dance record*

3. *Poster.*

4. *Ad company.*

5. *Poster promoting CD box collection.*

6. *CD box collection.*

7. *Tour poster.*

8. *Poster promoting record album.*

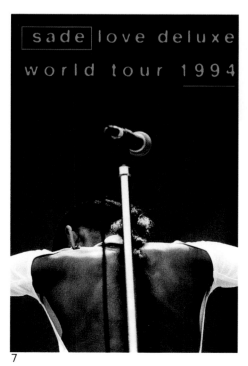

7

8

NORMAN MOORE DESIGN/ART, INC.

6311 Romaine Street, Los Angeles, CA 90038   213.467.2984   FAX 213.467.1985

1. *Design/Art logo.*
2. *Jazz record catalog.*
3. *Banner promoting record.*
4. *Font brochure.*
5. *CD cover.*

1

128

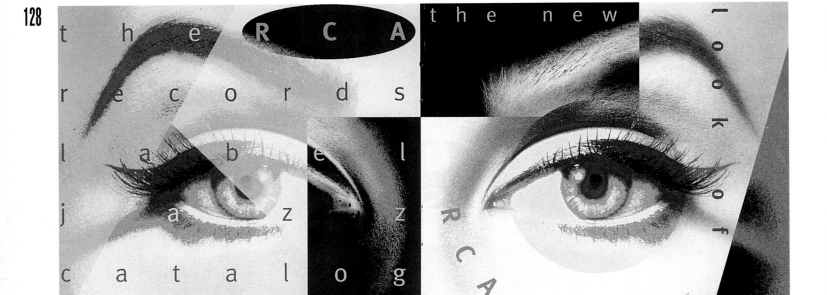

2

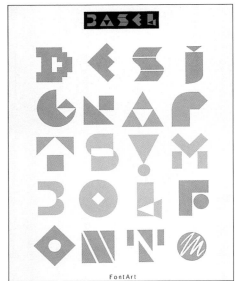

Andy Summers
new album
"synaesthesia"
out now on
CMP Records

3

4

FontArt

5

michael
osborne
design

Design is a process, a transformation of the abstract and undeveloped to the defined and informative. This process is creative and mental and there is no formula. Design is not a science.

Sometimes the process is a collaboration, sometimes an individual effort, in all cases the solutions should be appropriate. Every project presents new information, new problems and therefore new solutions. That is what drives Michael Osborne Design.

At Michael Osborne Design, there is no style guide. They look at every project from all perspectives, and have been doing so for over 15 years. Although their clients and projects are always diverse, the design principles remain the same. Design is a process and, for them, a passion.

1

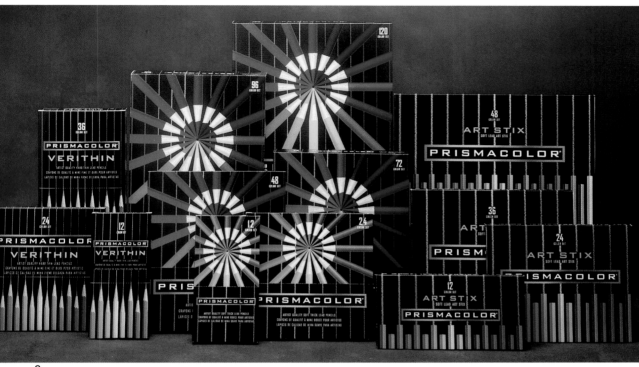

2

3

PHILHARMONIA
BAROQUE
ORCHESTRA

4

1. *Michael Osborne Design studio.*

2. *Sanford Corporation—Prismacolor:
The packaging system for the entire
line of Prismacolor art products was
created to further enhance the line's
premium image and appeal to a new
generation of users.*

3. *San Francisco Museum of Modern
Art—logo for in-store merchandise.*

4. *Philharmonia Baroque Orchestra—
corporate identity.*

5. *Sutter Home Winery—pasta sauce:
To leverage the taste appeal and
wonderful color of the sauces
themselves, this packaging uses a
clear label. It is branded with the
Sutter Home logo and uses an
illustration to further accentuate the
product's ingredients.*

6. *Nordstrom—Provencial Honey: An
earthy color palette with a central
bee illustration was used to convey
the integrity of this natural honey-
based home fragrance line.*

5

6

132

1

2

3

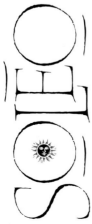

4   5

1. *Montevina Winery (Sutter Home Winery)—Terra d'Oro line: This unique bottle design captures the elegance of these traditional Italian varietals.*

2. *St. Stan's Brewery—Whistle Stop Ale: This pale ale is the latest addition to the microbrewery's product line.*

3. *Mumm Cuvée Napa (Seagram's Classics Wine Company)—DVX Origins: As a prototype blend, DVX Origins was packaged and sold in the tasting room only.*

4. *Sutter Home Winery—Soléo wine brand mark.*

5. *Cornerstone Cellars—Napa Valley Cabernet Sauvignon: This wine's label enables it to make a memorable first impression in the super-premium wine category.*

6. *Wente Vineyards—core line: Wente's new look bolsters its shelf presence, while alluding to the vineyard's longstanding heritage.*

134

1. *Knight-Ridder Information, Inc.— core line: To communicate the development of a new product line with a more user-friendly interface, a unique print collateral and packaging system was designed, including a retrofit to all existing materials.*

2. *ParaGraph Technologies—Virtual Home Space Builder: This authoring software for creating 3-D galleries for the World Wide Web uses packaging to help communicate the product's capabilities and ease-of-use.*

3. *Maxis—software publisher corporate identity.*

4. *StarPress Multimedia, Inc.— software publisher corporate identity.*

5. *Trancell Systems, Inc.—WebRamp: The brand identity, packaging and support collateral work as a system to communicate this product's all-in-one Internet accessibility for the small office environment.*

6. *Cardinal Technologies, Inc.— Fax/Modem: With its use of color and illustration, this package design achieves the approachability the company was after, while creating a strong billboarding effect on the retail shelf.*

7. *Skeleton Crew—computer reseller corporate identity.*

8. *Rocket Science—1996 product line brochure: This brochure captures the excitement and technical quality of the video games developed by this leading-edge producer.*

1

2

3

STARPRESS™
MULTIMEDIA

5

6

crew

skeleton

7

8

MICHAEL OSBORNE DESIGN
444 De Haro Street, Suite 207, San Francisco, CA 94107   415.255.0125   FAX 415.255.1312

1

the ACORN

3

2

1. *The Ansel Adams Gallery—
   newsletter masthead.*

2. *Meridian Industrial Trust—corporate
   identity, business system and
   annual report: This company needed
   a bold new identity to depict its
   prominent role in the industrial
   properties market. This look is
   carried through to the company's
   first annual report.*

3. *Chronicle Books—Sweet and
   Natural Baking: This collection of
   dessert recipes that use natural
   sugar substitutes was designed to
   capture the deliciousness and
   elegance available through this
   method of baking.*

4. *Della Hoss—broadsides: Della Hoss
   originally created these botanical
   and landscape woodcuts while
   living in the Yosemite area from
   1928 to 1942. The original art was
   digitally retouched and reproduced
   using letterpress printing.*

4

SF

yashi
okita
design

It's tough to tell which passion — golf or design — tugs at Yashi Okita more. The truth is, he approaches both with the same qualities.

On the course, he overcomes nature's complexity with a keen eye, clean swing and a burst of energy. The same is true of his alter-passion: clean, energetic designs to illustrate complex subjects.

After arriving in the United States in 1968, Yashi spent 15 years at advertising agencies as an art director and creative director. Directing other designers in developing his own concepts, though, was like asking a caddy to make your putt.

To get back to the hands-on work of mechanicals and drawing, he founded Yashi Okita Design in San Francisco in 1982 to focus on high-tech, consumer, medical and financial services companies. Today, his seven-person team spends about three-quarters of its time on traditional design, and the remainder on advertising.

In 25 years, Yashi is modestly proud of a portfolio that shines with award-winning designs for blue-chip clients. Now if he could only hit that first hole in one ...soon...

1

2

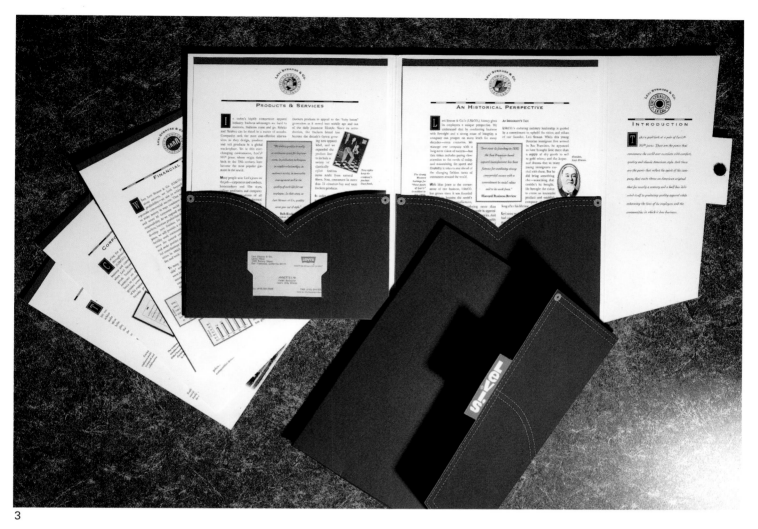

3

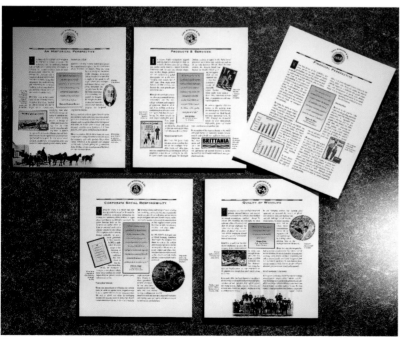

4

1. *Yashi Okita Design staff.*

2. *Studio logo.*

3-4. *Corporate materials for Levi Strauss & Co.*

1

2

1. *Proposal kit for Marriot Corporate Services.*

2. *Package design for Laserbyte Optical Disks.*

3-8. *Package design for Ed & Don's Chocolates.*

9. *Package design for Japonesk Chocolates.*

3

6

4

7

5

8

9

1

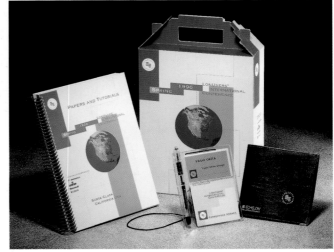

2

3

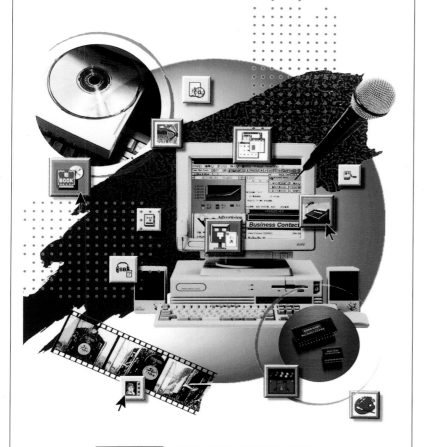

マルチメディアの世界に生きる旭化成の技術

ASAHI KASEI 旭化成マイクロシステム

4

5

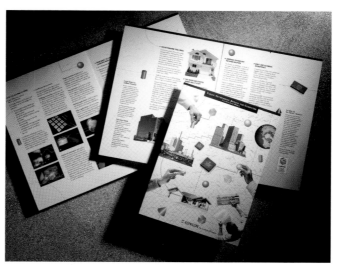

6

1-3. *Conference materials for Lonusers® International.*

4. *Poster for Asahi Kasei Microsystems.*

5. *Corporate brochure for AKM Semiconductor, Inc.*

6. *Corporate brochure for Echelon Corporation.*

1

2

3

5

4

144

1. *Yashi Okita Design promotional piece.*
2. *Signage for Courtyard Caffe.*
3. *Logo for Escort at Work.*
4. *Logo for Surelink.*
5. *Package design for Maxoptix Optical Disks.*

Ph.D

LA

146

Everything. It's what P*h*.D designers Michael Hodgson and Clive Piercy did for their largest project to date—an office chair from renowned furniture designer Don Chadwick. They gave the chair an identity, named it (evo), designed promotional and marketing materials, created packaging, showrooms, brochures, print ads, point-of-purchase displays and even directed a promotional film. "The evo project clearly illustrated the scope of our interests," says Clive. "Variety excites us."

This fascination with all aspects of design enables P*h*.D to devise solutions that are neither obvious or predictable. Michael explains, "When we're asked to create an exhibit booth (the recent Virgin Interactive Entertainment installation), produce motion graphics or design a book jacket, we're able to tap into what we've learned from other realms, whether it be empathy for the written word, or sensitivity to three dimensions."

Although born and bred in England (where, according to Clive, even toilet paper advertising is thoughtfully produced) both men are self-avowed americanophiles. Each traveled to Los Angeles with a strong belief in tradition—to which they hold fast—to be liberated by the looser and more easygoing American style. While Clive and Michael describe themselves as polar opposites, together they produce work that is charming and clever. In fact, a thread of humor winds its' way into many of their designs, beginning with the firm's name. "P*h*.D is a bit of a pompous name for a company," laughs Hodgson. "We were being tongue-in-cheek and serious at the same time." Which, as is often the case with P*h*.D's design, says everything.

1

2

3

4

5

6

7

8

9

10

Ph.D, circa 1951

11

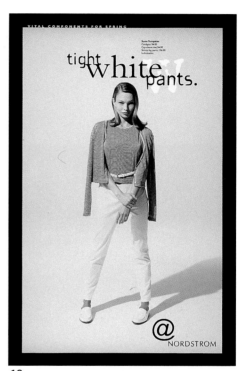

12

13

1-10. *Logos.*

1. *Editing facility.*

2. *Ashland & Hill, furniture store.*

3. *Commercial production company.*

4. *Evans/Foden, production design.*

5. *Editing house.*

6. *Coyne Operated, commercial production company.*

7. *Software development campus.*

8. *Sound design and editing company.*

9. *Landscape architect.*

10. *Ergonomic office chair manufactured by Herman Miller.*

11-12. *Regional advertising campaign.*

13. *Design for a series of golf ads. Client: Wieden and Kennedy.*

148

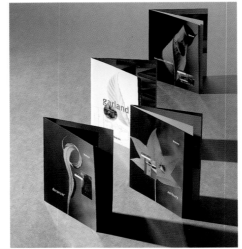

4

2

3

5

1

6

7

1-3. *"Digital Junkyard" exhibition space for Virgin Interactive. Design and implementation.*

4. *Brochure series for Steelcase.*

5. *Modular packaging system.*

6. *Photography promotion.*

7. *Advertising campaign for swimwear manufacturer.*

8-10. *Brochures for software development campus.*

11. *Identity for architectural tour, to benefit Santa Monica AIDS Project.*

12. *Identity for local charity 5-10K run.*

8

9

10

11

12

150

1

2

3

4

5

1-3. *CD covers for Quango Music.*

4. *Signage for community arts project.*

5-6. *Brochure for sportswear designer and manufacturer.*

7. *Educational cable channel identity.*

8-9. *Cookery books.*

10. *Advertising agency identity.*

7

8

9

10

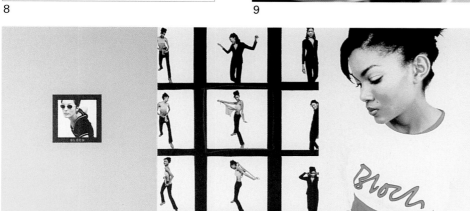

6

P *h* . D
1524a Cloverfield Blvd., Santa Monica, CA 90404   310.829.0900   Fax: 310.829.1859

152

Motion graphics

1-2. *AT&T commercials.*
Director: David Fincher.

3. *1-800-DENTIST commercial,*
design and art direction.

4. *Nike commercial.*
Director: David Fincher.

5. *Direction and design of promotional*
video for Herman Miller.

6. *Madonna music video.*
Director: Mark Romanek.

SF

profile
design

Quality design is a blend of creative passion and marketing discipline. This philosophy brought Russ Baker, Tom McNulty and Kenichi Nishiwaki together to establish Profile Design more than eight years ago. "Our approach to design simply means translating each client's marketing objectives into visual solutions— the result of listening intently to our clients," says Tom, whose innovative spirit is reflected in his role as the firm's brand and packaging expert.

154

Born and raised in Japan, Kenichi brings an astute cross-cultural sensibility to design. Kenichi's knowledge of international markets serves clients well when designing their corporate identity programs. "We encourage the dynamic exchange of ideas in our studio, which makes for an exciting and energetic environment," he says.

"Intelligently planned and professionally executed graphic design reduces time to market and greatly increases a product's potential for success," says Russ, whose talent for creating momentum is invaluable to mission-critical projects.

As a hands-on, unified team, Profile achieves its goals with integrity, imagination and delight. Specialists in brand and corporate identity, packaging, and marketing collateral, Profile Design has generated solid business design solutions for clients such as Dole Food Company, The Coca-Cola Company, Kikkoman International and Intel Corporation.

1

2

Photo, left to right: *Lena Tønseth, Jeanne Namkung, Jill Knowles, Anthony Luk, Joseph DiMeo, Susan Stein, Brian Jacobson, Tom McNulty, Toiya Lumley, Gary Siu, Nicole Lanzotti, Eileen Carey, Russ Baker, and Kenichi Nishiwaki (seated).*

3

4

5

6

9

1. *Studio logo.*

2. *Profile Design staff.*

3. *Design studio.*

4. *Package design for Schneider beer.*

5. *Brand identity for DiNapoli canned goods.*

6. *Package design for DiNapoli canned tomatoes.*

7. *Corporate identity for Project Open Hand, a non-profit organization.*

8. *Brand identity for Dr. McDougall's Right Foods Company.*

9. *Package design for Dr. McDougall's Right Foods instant cup meals.*

10. *Package design for Stock Pot soups, sauces and gravies.*

10

PROJECT
Open Hand

7

156

1

2

3

4

5

6

7

8

9

10

1. *Package design for Jimmie's Asian Cuisine frozen foods.*

2. *Brand identity for Sun Brew iced teas.*

3. *Package design for Hinode Rice Bowl frozen entrées.*

4. *Brand identity for Apple-Apple.*

5. *Package design for Apple-Apple fruit juices.*

6. *Retail packaging program for Carneros Alambic Distillery.*

7. *Poster for Otis Spunkmeyer's food service and sales program.*

8. *Package design for Otis Spunkmeyer's frozen cookie dough.*

9. *Package design for Otis Spunkmeyer's muffins.*

10. *Package design for Santa Cruz Fine Foods Salad Eatos.*

11. *Brand identity for Razal popcorn.*

12. *Brand identity for the Mariani Nut Company.*

11

12

ASCEND

1

158

2

3

1. *Corporate identity for Ascend Communications, Inc.*

2. *Annual report design for Ascend.*

3. *Sales support kit for Ascend.*

4. *Promotional material for Ascend's Pipeline 25 ISDN product launch.*

5. *Package and manual design for First Virtual Corporation's Media Operating Software.*

6. *Package design for SBT Accounting Systems' software programs.*

7. *Corporate identity for Lifespring personal transformation workshops.*

8. *Identity applications for Lifespring.*

9. *Newsletter design for Lifespring.*

10. *Corporate identity for FutureTel, Inc.*

11. *Corporate identity for Strategy Manufacturing.*

12. *Event identity to promote the California Countryside Festival.*

13. *Identity for the Four Seasons Piano Bar.*

14. *Event identity for the International Association of Business Communicators.*

4

5

6

Lifespring

7

8

9

FutureTel

10

STRATEGY

11

CALIFORNIA
CounTrysidE
FesTivaL

12

FOUR SEASONS
PIANO BAR

13

14

1

2

1. *Cover of the Kikkoman International Teriyaki brochure.*

2. *Inside spread of the Kikkoman International Teriyaki brochure.*

3. *Brochure design for Elo Touchsystems interactive computer screens.*

4. *Brochure design for TraceTek Raychem Corporation's leak detection system.*

5. *Brochure for Intel's Pentium Processor.*

3

4

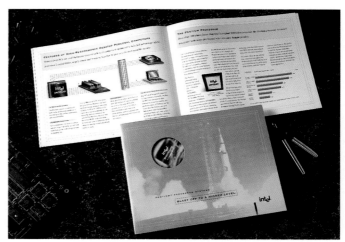

5

160

sackett
design
associates

162 Founded in 1988, Sackett Design Associates has become a highly regarded, award-winning design and marketing communications company. Their multi-disciplinary firm's clients include large corporations as well as small start-up companies. Headquartered in San Francisco, Sackett Design Associates has a staff of seven designers and account management personnel. They own and occupy two buildings in the Pacific Heights neighborhood of San Francisco which house not only the company's operations, but approximately seventy collections of antique toys, game boards, packaging, and advertising items. Sackett Design Associates also operates a satellite office out of Kansas City.

Mark Sackett, the principal owner and creative director, and his staff have won over 450 industry awards in national and international design competitions. Their work has been published in numerous design annuals, books, and publications. Additionally, their work is included in the permanent collections of the Library of Congress and the Association for Computing Machinery.

Sackett Design Associates selects assignments in which they can collaborate with their clients in the creation of strategic dynamic solutions to increase sales, market share, and visibility. In addition, they have designed and implemented a creativity training program entitled Brainfood™ for corporations with in-house creative departments focusing primarily on team building, research techniques, motivational programs, and exercises designed to improve an individual's productivity as well as their creative product.

Client: AMCAL
Project: "The Artful Garden"
Calendar and Note Cards
Created in collaboration with Holly Stewart Photography, utilizing Sackett Design's vast antique and ephemera collections as props.

Sackett Design Associates
From left to right:
James Sakamoto,
Wayne Sakamoto,
Mark Sackett

Client: AR Lithographers

Project: New Year's Poster

This two-sided, self-promotion poster for AR Lithographers showcases various printing techniques and alludes to holiday stresses in a humorous manner.

Client: Theory of Cool

Project: CD Stacking System

Mark Sackett and his staff drew from their frustrated experience at trying to find consistent storage for their compact disc collections and created this completely modular system that locks together. The system is sold at music and furniture stores nationwide.

Client: Jossey-Bass Inc., Publishers

Project: Book Jacket

This book cover for "The Leadership Challenge" capitalizes on the reputations of its authors, and creates a powerful shelf presence.

164

Client: Mind Care

Project: Naming/Corporate Identity/Business Papers System

Sackett Design developed not only the graphics system, but the name for this company that conducts business and creativity seminars offered to executives experiencing career burnout.

Client: Levi Strauss & Co.

Project: Calendar/Poster

As an in-house call to action for an employee program entitled "Get it Right," this Calendar/Poster illustrates the proper rules to follow when using the Levi Strauss & Co. brand marks.

Client: Full Moon Foods
and Mercantile

Project: Corporate
Identity/Packaging

The identity for this
organic market was created
to function not only as the
business cards, but as the
entire packaging, price tag
and promotions system,
allowing the market to
open quickly and
inexpensively.

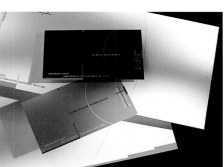

Client: Bourret Pearlman
Architecture Design Studio

Project: Corporate Identity/
Business Papers System

Sackett Design's architects
required a new identity system
that would reflect not only the
principals' styles, but their equal
representation within the firm.

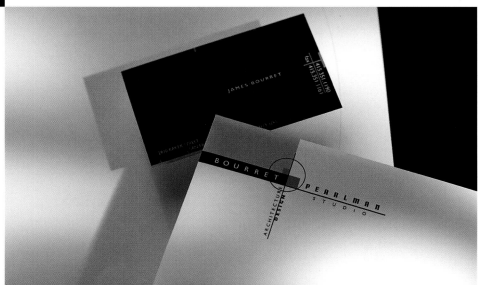

166

Client: UtiliCorp United

Project: Corporate Book
and Portfolio

*This signed, limited edition
book, portfolio and slip-case
traces the history of the
American utility business.
The book and folio contain
sixteen hand-tipped-in
illustrations. The slipcase
allows UtiliCorp to
customize each book, which
is used as a corporate gift.*

Client: The Hard Way

Project: Concept/Product
Development

*Designs for "The Hard
Way," a new licensing
concept designed for
application to apparel,
snowboards, and various
trends product.*

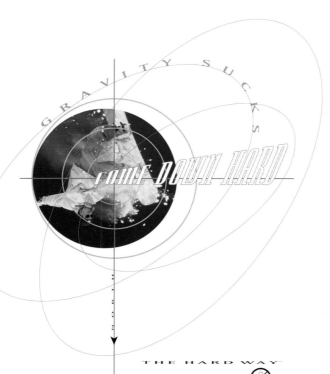

Client: Sprint

Project: Image Brochure

This brochure, for the business division of Sprint, utilizes customer testimonials and a time line to illustrate Sprint's capabilities and global presence.

Client: Sprint

Project: Vertical Market Brochures

This series of brochures was designed to communicate Sprint's unique business solutions for specific market segments such as health care, manufacturing, and international business.

Client: Shawnee Mission North High School

Project: Class of 1975 Reunion Poster

Mark Sackett did not want his high school reunion to pass by without some memento, so he designed and donated this two-sided, six-color poster as a gift to each class member.

168

Client: Matt and Angela Sackett

Project: Birth Announcement

This semi-official IRS looking document capitalizes not only on the April 15th birthdate of Mark Sackett's niece, but also on the fact that the child's mother is an accountant.

Client: Firefighters in the Schools

Project: Logo

"Firefighters in the Schools" is a non-profit program that teaches fire safety to children. Sackett Design created the firefly as the official mascot of the program to enhance the appeal to children.

Client: Ira K. Glasser

Project: Corporate Identity/Business Papers System

Ira Glasser, a creativity management consultant, needed an identity system that conceptually communicated his unique consulting approach to his financial and real estate client base.

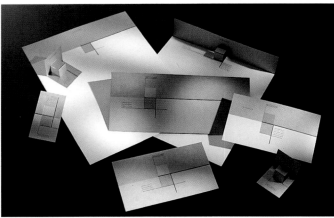

Client: Sackett Design Associates

Project: Christmas Card

Sackett Design makes an annual Christmas donation to a charity that has some timely relevance to members of its staff. This 1995 holiday card tells their annual story and benefits the American Cancer Society.

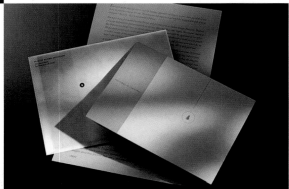

sargent
&
berman

LA

170 Founded in 1987, Sargent & Berman has emerged as a leading design firm specializing in packaging, corporate identity and marketing communications.

Principals Peter Sargent and Greg Berman lead a team of designers in solving creative problems for a wide range of clients in industries as diverse as toys, cruise lines and healthcare. The underlying philosophy of Sargent & Berman's work is that no single style is appropriate for every assignment. Whether designing a brochure or a package, identity or ad, the solutions are geared toward addressing the specific needs of the client rather than adhering to a single established aesthetic. This allows for more creativity to explore different ideas rather than relying on a standard approach.

While much of their client base is local, they service an increasing number of national clients based outside of Southern California, and routinely compete with other major national firms for business.

With offices located on the Third Street Promenade in Santa Monica, their work reflects the diverse energy of the area, as well as providing a fun and creative environment for staff and visiting clients.

Sargent & Berman's staff is comprised of a mix of approximately 15 full-time and freelance designers trained in traditional methods as well as being proficient in state-of-the-art digital technology.

1

2

3

1. *Pep Products Pocket Rocket packaging.*

2. *Sunkist Fruit Roll food packaging.*

3. *Marcus Oliver men's hair care packaging line.*

172

1

2

3

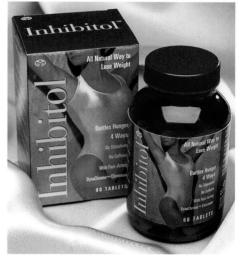

6

1. *Princess Cruises travel agent window display.*

2. *Princess Cruises past passenger newsletters.*

3. *Princess Cruises sales support materials.*

4. *Garden of Paradise bath & massage product line.*

5. *St. John's Hospital Annual Report.*

6. *Pep Products Inhibitol dietary supplement.*

4

5

174

1

2

3

1. *Coca-Cola Clothing promotional mailing.*

2. *Anderson Printing prepress promotional and sales materials.*

3. *Czarskaya Vodka ultra premium brand.*

4

5

6

4. *Advance Travel Management corporate identity program.*

5. *Breaking Away Cycling Tour corporate identity program.*

6. *UCSF Mount Zion Medical Center corporate identity program.*

7. *The Franklin Mint corporate identity program.*

8. *Marcus Oliver corporate identity program.*

9. *Boyer Sport identification for sports apparel.*

10. *Florida Hospital corporate identity program.*

11. *Princess Cruises Ship corporate identity program for "Sun Princess."*

12. *Tool Box corporate identity program.*

7

8

9

10

11

12

176

1

2

3

4

5

1. *Saban's Power Rangers Zeo logo for a television program.*

2. *Saban's Beetleborgs logo for a television program.*

3. *Creative Critters product packaging for childrens' electronic products.*

4. *Bandai America product packaging for Power Rangers and Power Rangers Zeo toy lines.*

5. *Bandai America product packaging for The Tick toy line.*

michael
schwab
studio

SF

178 Originally from Oklahoma, Michael Schwab has become one of the leading graphic artists in the United States.

Having gone to school in Texas, New York, and Los Angeles, Michael has an extensive breadth of visual and natural references to which he continually turns for ideas. After graduating from L.A.'s Art Center College of Design, Michael moved to Marin County in northern California where he and his wife, photographer Kathryn Kleinman, and their sons now live.

Michael's work is known for its large, flat areas of color, dramatic perspectives, and bold, graphic images of archetypal people. Often working from posed models, taking polaroids and designing in front of the camera to achieve the lines and shadows he wants, the result appears highly disciplined, but with the pain of effort invisible.

His work is eye-catching in its simplicity.

Michael's positive attitude and energy continue to keep him one step ahead of the demands of his fast paced career. He has created national award-winning logos and posters for many clients including Apple, Levi's, Coke, Reebok, Polo Ralph Lauren, Lexus, The Golden Gate National Parks and the San Francisco Opera.

Michael Schwab is now winning awards in every major graphic design and illustration show in the United States, and is being featured in publications worldwide.

1

ALCATRAZ

2

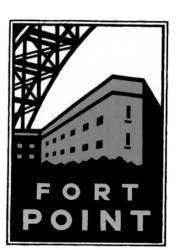

FORT POINT

3

MUIR WOODS

4

1-4. *The Golden Gate National Parks: These images appeared in the San Francisco area as bus shelter posters as well as at the various parks.*
Art director: Rich Silverstein, Jami Spittler 1996.

180

1. *Cowboy: This poster is a four-color serigraph.*
   Art director: Ken Slazyc 1995.

2. *Join Up: Recruitment poster created for the rowing team at Oklahoma State University.*
   Art director: Paul Schwab 1990.

2

182

THE GOLDEN GATE NATIONAL PARKS

Larry Mahan

B O O T S

PATRICO-SINARE

6th Annual Polo Classic: A six-color,
silkscreen printed poster.
Art director: William Merriken 1995.

184 *APL Poster: Serigraph created for the 1996 American Presidents Line calendar/poster.*
Art director: Andy Dreyfus 1995.

shimokochi/
reeves

LA

186

"Dramatic graphics yield dramatic results," asserts Anne Reeves, Vice President/Director of Marketing of Shimokochi/Reeves. Her view that "packaging is everything" is substantiated by a track record of helping clients increase sales through bold visual designs. Whether it's television station identities, vitamin lines or even hotel collateral, the company believes the presentation of a corporate/brand image must be strong, immediate and memorable. "That's the fastest way to translate a client's marketing objectives into bottom line results," she says.

According to Mamoru Shimokochi, President/Creative Director of Shimokochi/Reeves, "We view every package as a billboard." That's especially important since 90% of the product lines they work on are sold in competitive store environments where shelf impact and shopability are critical. This strong visual impact at the point of purchase has helped a number of clients achieve dramatic sales increases, without any consumer advertising.

Founded in 1985, Shimokochi/Reeves is headed by Mamoru Shimokochi and Anne Reeves. They've earned a reputation for developing highly marketable solutions that lead to extraordinary sales results for well established brands and new product launches. Highly experienced, with a broad range of international clients, Shimokochi/Reeves' compact size allows for clear lines of communication, with clients receiving close personal attention from both partners and the entire staff. Their long term relationships with clients in the food, health & beauty, industrial, financial and entertainment categories amplify the idea that results-oriented design translates to success in the marketplace.

1

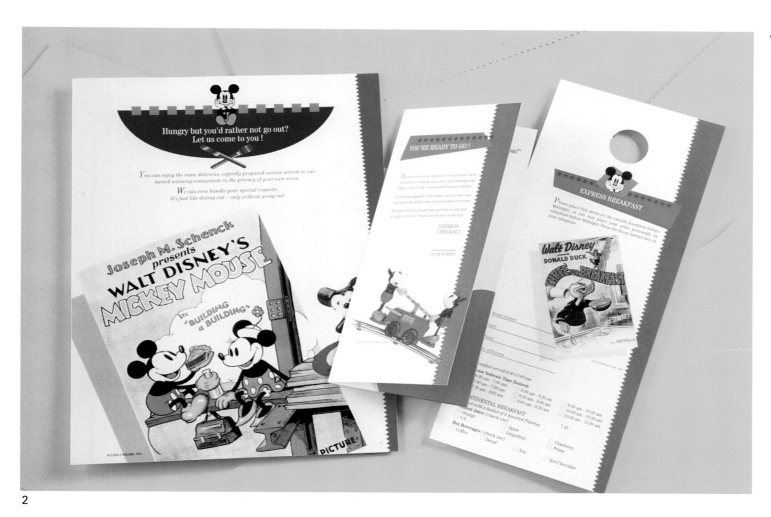

2

3

1. S/R Marketing Man Watch: Christmas promotion.

2-3. Disneyland: system of marketing materials for Disneyland's Pacific Hotel.

188

1

2

3

4

1. *Noodles & Sauce: brand & package identity for Nissin Foods' new product introduction.*

2. *Stuffovers: name development, brand & package identity.*

3. *Las Campanas Taquitos: packaging for a line of high quality taquitos.*

4. *Tokyo Broadcasting System (TBS): corporate identity program.*

5-6. *Kagoshima: proposed symbols for the Prefecture of Kagoshima, Japan.*

7. *The Safari Golf Co.: symbol for a line of golf apparel.*

8. *UCLA – School of Theater, Film & Television (TFT).*

9. *X-Century Studios: identity for a multi-media center.*

10. *IZEN: logotype/symbol for a textile design company.*

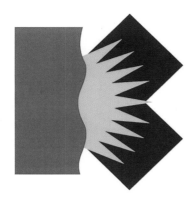

5

6

7

U C L A

SCHOOL OF THEATER
FILM AND TELEVISION

8

9

10

190

1. *Professional Solutions: new product development, identity and packaging.*

2. *Topol Plus: brand & package identity.*

3. *La Moy: upscale packaging for a skin care line.*

4. *Murad – Vitamin Supplements: packaging for a new upscale line of advanced "skin care" vitamin supplements.*

1

2

3

4

5

5. *Bodycology: brand identity and package re-design for 33 body, bath & hair care products.*

6. *Your Life Vitamins: package revitalization for the "Your Life" lifestyle multi-vitamins.*

6

192

1

2

1. *Nature's Family: brand identity & package revitalization for a line of natural ingredient based skin care products.*

2. *L.A. Looks: new product development (brand name & packaging) targeted at the youth-oriented market.*

patrick
soohoo
designers

LA

194 Patrick SooHoo Designers has built a standard for excellence with a demanding philosophy of marketing-based design and result-oriented creative.

The award-winning PSH team specializes in advertising, promotions, packaging, merchandising and corporate identity. Their diverse client list ranges from entertainment and financial industries to consumer goods and business-to-business marketing. PSH has also expanded services offering outstanding marketing and creative programs in multiple languages.

Patrick SooHoo Designers has built long-term client relationships and established new ones with a simple philosophy: Success starts with a sound strategic approach and results in an impactful, seamless message.

As Patrick SooHoo says, "We design solutions. Creative solutions that meet marketing and communication objectives. Simply. Effectively. Uniquely. If our work meets those goals, clients will buy it, consumers will react to it, and all involved will be successful."

1

2

3

4

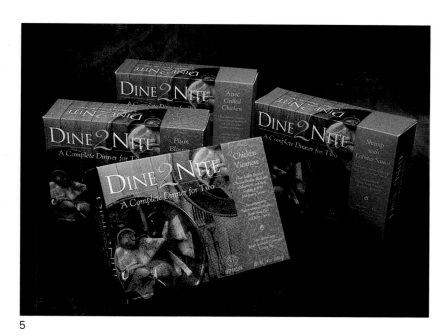

5

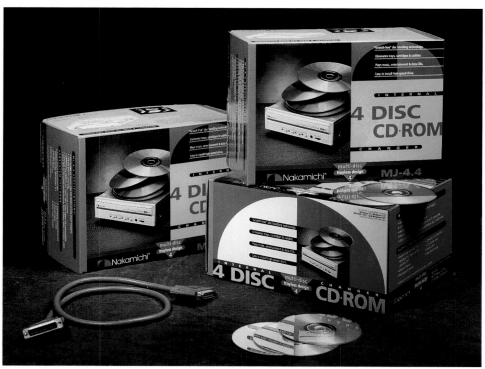

6

1. *Patrick SooHoo design team.*

2. *Trademark for Apollo '96.*

3. *Self-promotion.*

4. *Limited edition Barbie packaging for Mattel sold at FAO Schwarz stores.*

5. *Food packaging for Overhill Farms.*

6. *Retail packaging for Nakamichi America Corporation.*

196

Ontario
Southern California

1

2

3

L.A. Care
HEALTH PLAN

5

4

1. *Trademark for Ontario Convention and Visitors Bureau.*

2. *Product brochure for Epson America Inc.*

3-4. *Point-of-sale displays for Epson America Inc.*

5. *Trademark for L.A. Care, Local Initiative Health Authority for L.A. County.*

6. *Licensing style guide for Mattel's Hot Wheels.*

6

198

1

1-5. *Trademarks and collateral materials for an insurance company's sales incentive programs.*

2

SALZBURG
CZECH INTO

3

4

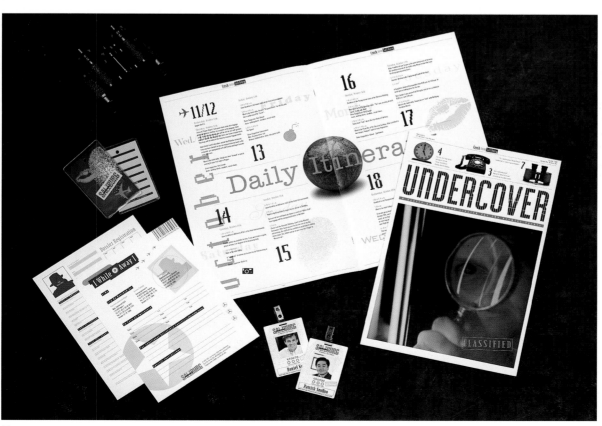

5

200

1

3

2

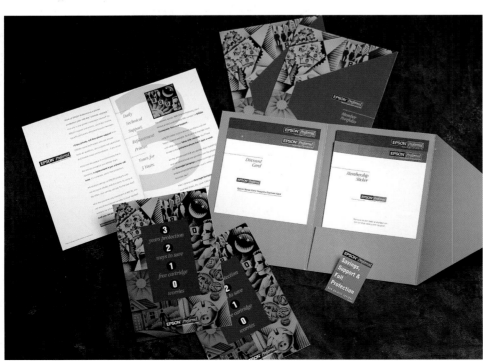

4

1-2. *"Winnie the Pooh" promotional program for Mattel Inc.*

3. *Promotional symbol for Primestar Television.*

4. *Extended warranty program for Epson America Inc.*

vrontikis
design
office

LA

CAFE La Bohème

204

1-4. *Details of invitations and plates from Cafe La Boheme, Monsoon Cafe, and Zest.*

5. *Examples of identities and printed materials for restaurants in Tokyo and Los Angeles. Clockwise: Cafe La Boheme, Tableaux, Monsoon Cafe, Jackson's, and Zest.*

6. *Poster for the opening of the second Monsoon Cafe in Tokyo.*

1

5

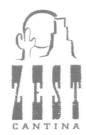
ZEST
CANTINA

2

3

4

TABLEAUX

MONSOON
CAFE

Jacksons

6

7

8

9

10

11

12

7. *Printer and paper company promotions: (clockwise) a series of Syquest covers, floppy disk holders and decimal conversion charts for Donahue Printing in Los Angeles illustrating various techniques on tree-free paper stocks; holiday cards for Donahue Printing; "Multiple Exposures from Lithographix," a quarterly exhibition of images from top photographers geared to designers and art directors.*

8. *"Now is Not the Time to Compromise" is #4 in a series of personal essays by leading graphic designers on the tension between integrity and compromise for Potlatch Paper Company, Cloquet, Minnesota.*

9-12. *Innovatively-packaged gift tag collections given each holiday season to clients and friends of Vrontikis Design Office. Shown here: the 1992 - 1995 promotions.*

1

1. *Marketing materials and identity for the Industry Advantage Health Plans of the Motion Picture and Television Fund (a Blue Cross of California HMO).*

2. *Various identities and marketing materials for health care clients, including Childrens Hospital Los Angeles; The Arthritis Center; The San Fernando Valley Fertility and Reproductive Center; other specializations of Encino/Tarzana Regional Medical Center.*

3. *Identity for the San Fernando Valley Heart Institute.*

4. *Annual reports for the ARCO Foundation.*

2

4

3

5

6

5. *Detail of the Harvey Mason "Ratamacue" CD package for Atlantic Records.*

6. *Clockwise: packaging and press kit for "Great Legends of Song" a 32-CD series presenting highlights from the archives of Capitol Records; poster and catalog for: "A Tribute to Antonio Carlos Jobim" (Avery Fischer Hall, N.Y.); and CD packaging for jazz percussionist Harvey Mason.*

7. *Promotional materials for the nationally televised 2nd Annual Screen Actors Guild Awards, including the invitation, award certificate, and program.*

8. *Detail of the Capitol Records "Great Legend of Song" collection.*

7

8

208

1. *Identity, stationery, and press kit for Unitel Video's Playpen division, which produces video entertainment graphics for television and film.*

2. *Identity for Greenhood and Company, new media "construction" experts.*

3. *Innovative special event promotional materials for "Making Sense of It," a five-day sales meeting for Avery Dennison, each day of which focused on one of the senses.*

1

3

2

Photography: Paul Ottengheime

the
warren
group

LA

210

Balance any number of elements at one time. Do it so well the effort is indiscernible. Art and copy. Typography and visual detail. Message and medium. Countless decisions go into creating design that doesn't simply dress up the page, but communicates. That's what The Warren Group strives for.

One key to their success is collaboration. Working from their Venice USA studio, they assemble the best possible creative team for each project, which may include art directors, illustrators, photographers, copywriters and Web artists. One hallmark of their style is an inventive use of illustration. They are always pushing the boundaries and seeking out the most original work.

The Warren Group is happy to note others have recognized the results. Since their inception in 1984, they have won awards from such groups as the Art Directors Clubs of Los Angeles and New York, American Center for Design, American Institute of Graphic Arts, and the International Association of Business Communicators. More importantly, they have a contented and expanding client list.

The Warren Group's work has been selected for the Library of Congress Permanent Collection. That means you can see their balancing act in the nation's capital. Or you can see it in Venice, CA.

1

1. *The studio with Phoebe.*

2-5. *A quarterly magazine for the University of Southern California School of Medicine.*

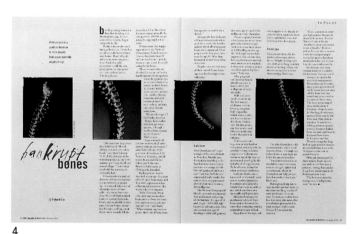

212

1

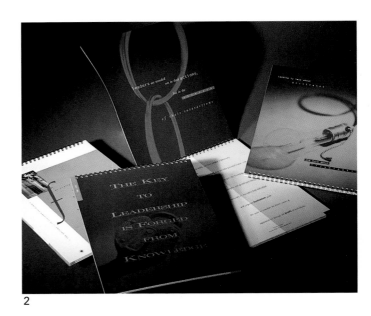

2

1. *Book jacket for Norton Books.*

2. *Fall catalog for the University of Southern California Office of Executive Development.*

3. *Collateral materials for the Apple Worldwide conference. Logo design by Ed Hynes of Troon, Ltd.*

3

6

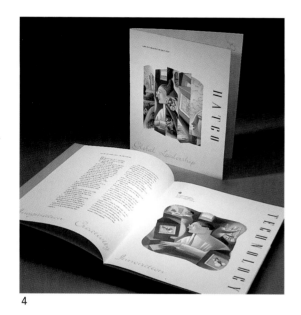

4

Catfish Farms
studio

7

5

4. *Capabilities brochure for Hatco, a specialty chemicals manufacturer.*

5. *Fall catalog for Harvard-Westlake School, an exclusive middle and upper school.*

6. *Logo for a total body maintenance firm, Performance Fitness Concepts.*

7. *Symbol for a photographic and digital studio, Catfish Farms.*

214

1

1-3. *Aqueduct 2000, a bi-monthly magazine for the Metropolitan Water District of Southern California.*

4. *Studio self-promotion, "Design Mathematics."*

5. *"Hit the Road," a travel journal published as a specialty retail gift item and self-promotion.*

6. *An annual awards booklet honoring the year's outstanding employees of Mattel.*

7. *Symbol for an Italian restaurant, Crostini.*

8. *Symbol for Creative Wonder, an events production company.*

9. *Fiftieth anniversary logo for Tektronix, Inc. of Wilsonville, Oregon.*

2

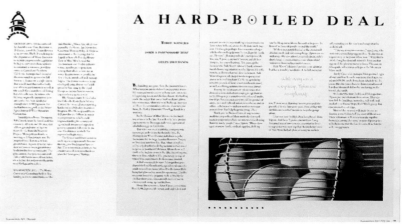

3

4

5

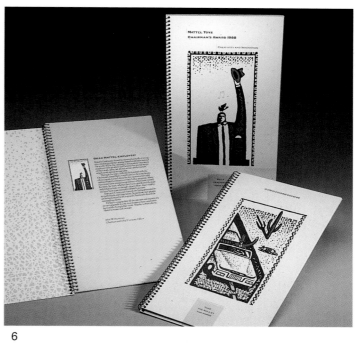

6

7

Creative Wonder

8

9

216

Baby of Mine
FAMILY CHILDBIRTH CENTER

1

3-4

2

1. *Recruitment package for IVI Publishing.*

2. *Book design for the Society of Illustrators of Los Angeles annual show.*

3-4. *Logo and collateral materials for Tri-Cities Medical Center family childbirth center. Developed in conjunction with ProMedica, International.*

white
design

LA

218

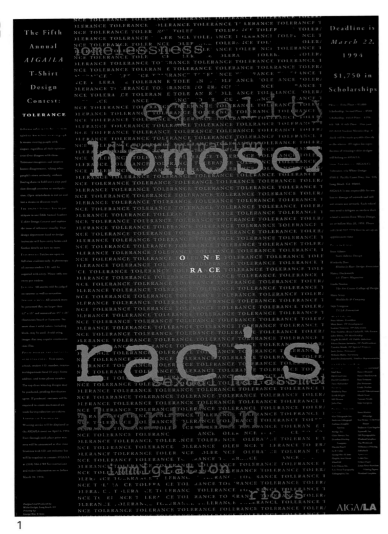

1

2

3

Change (in the design industry). If you're not uncomfortable, you should be. Why? Because we can't fully discern the impact of new technologies, yet we must keep up with them. Because a single area of specialization will no longer do. And because, as in any other business, the bottom line must be reached quickly.

Change (internal). White Design is shifting gears and branching out. Adding more depth to its client service. Changing job descriptions to allow people to move into areas where they can extend themselves and grow. The solution develops from several layers of expertise — marketing, design, account management and production. It's a more efficient way to work, the result of an ongoing process of change.

Change (in client relationships). Clients want more services and they want them faster. The rewards, if you are responsive, are full-scale marketing programs instead of individual projects, and bigger clients. White Design is targeting clients who understand the role of design in marketing com-munications, and who value integrity in these super-competitive times. That is what doesn't change.

4

1. *AIGA Student Design Contest poster for "Tolerance" theme.*

2. *White Design calling card promotion.*

3. *Lobby of White Design.*

4. *Isuzu sporting event promotional logo.*

5. *Celebrity Golf Championship poster for Isuzu.*

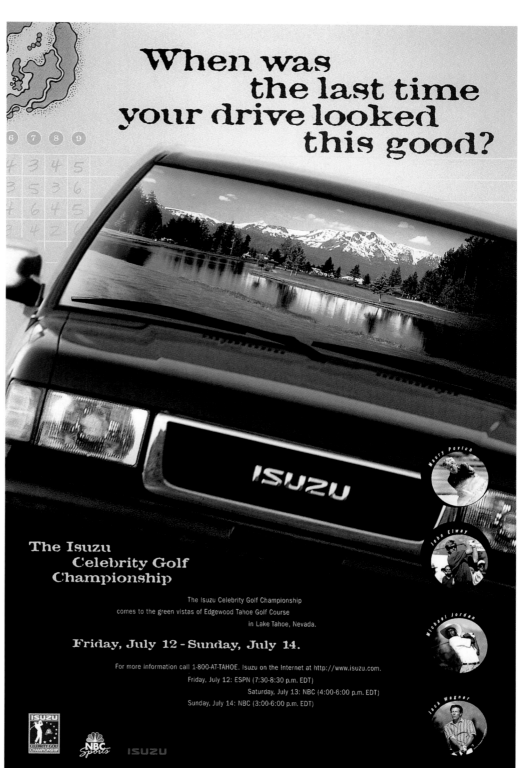

5

220

2

1

3

4

1. *Direct marketing program for L.A. Cellular Digital SST.*

2. *Free-standing point-of-purchase display.*

3-4. *L.A. Cellular Superstore interior.*

5. *Sponsorship clothing for cycling team.*

6. *L.A. Cellular AVP CA volleyball tour promotion.*

5

6

222

1

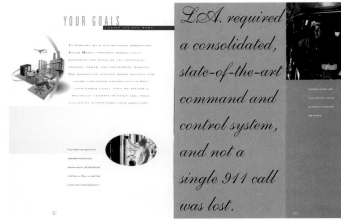

2

1-2. *Fluor Daniel Worldwide capabilities brochure.*

3-5. *1995 Annual Report for Quarterdeck.*

Corporate Identity For:

6. *Southern California Edison Energy Efficiency and Marketing Services Division.*

7. *Legal consultants for a business and engineering firm.*

8. *Guadalupe Home, a safe haven for abused and homeless children.*

9. *National Physicians Network, a multi-specialty medical group.*

10. *A private club/restaurant.*

11. *Isuzu Drive for '95.*

12. *A mediated dispute resolution law firm.*

13. *A securities brokerage firm.*

14. *Commons Restaurant located on USC campus.*

3

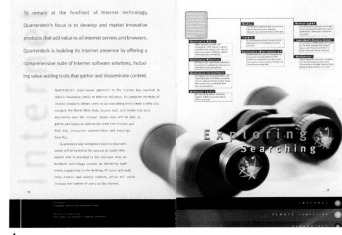

4

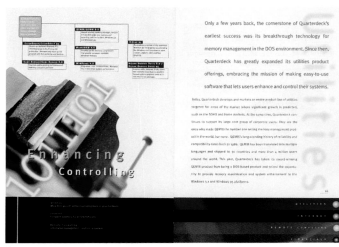

5

6

B

Barrington

7

223

8

9

MADELEINE'S

10

11

BFK&M

12

Pacific Coast
Financial Securities

13

14

224

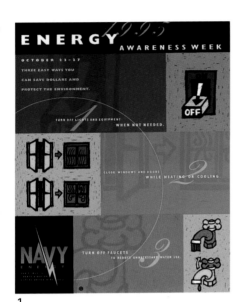

1

2

3

1-2. *Navy Energy Awareness Week poster and exhibit.*

3. *CD Packaging and promotional material.*

4. *Southern California Edison spare refrigerator recycling program.*

4

SF

zimmermann
crowe
design

226 Is graphic design a linear or non-linear process? That could be the topic of discussion for a busload of high brow designers. But the *business* of graphic design, at least according to Dennis Crowe and Neal Zimmermann, is definitely linear in nature, where past projects become the ladder rungs upon which they stand to reach their next goal.

Their extensive work in retail merchandising programs led them to direct and produce edgy in-store image videos as a component of the retail environment. The videos led to designing and directing television spots for MTV and Levi Strauss & Co. The television work became the stepping stones to film projects with Colossal Pictures and Touchstone Pictures.

"The progression is exciting, the unexpected twists in the road propel us forward, and give us an ever-expanding creative bag of capabilities to offer our clients," says Zimmermann.

Dennis and Neal are quick to credit their top-notch staff of designers, project managers and business administrators for operating efficiently and intelligently. The working atmosphere at their studio is unpretentious and relaxed, yet productive.

"San Francisco is an ideal location for graphic design," says Crowe, "where cultural influence and client sophistication blend to form a stimulating creative environment."

ZCD created a fresh yet classic look for the Levi's® 501® for Women point of purchase campaign. The pared-down blue tone photographs shot by Matthew Rolston are prominently featured on posters and 12" x 12" cubes.

228

*Designed for heavy airplay on the MTV
network, this spot is an intentionally
busy parade of strangeness that continues
to entertain, even when in heavy rotation.
Inspired by everyone from Magritte
to Fellini, this combination of live-action
and stop-motion animation was
conceived, designed and directed by ZCD
and produced by Colossal Pictures.*

This new virtual reality software revolutionized VR programming by allowing the easy manipulation of elements in real time. ZCD created all elements of the product launch including the packaging, (seen here) the product name and graphic identity (with interchangeable dual gender iterations) among other items.

230

1

The Levi's® Heritage Retail Shop
was designed to leverage Levi's®
long, rich history and significance
as the original jeansmaker into a
visually exciting, well structured
shopping environment. From
fixture, poster and signage design
to the use of specially treated and
aged materials, ZCD created a
complete retail statement which
strengthens the Levi's® brand and
reinforces the company's unique
stake in history.

2

3

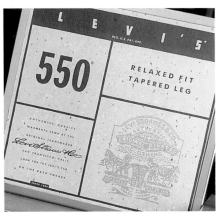

4

5

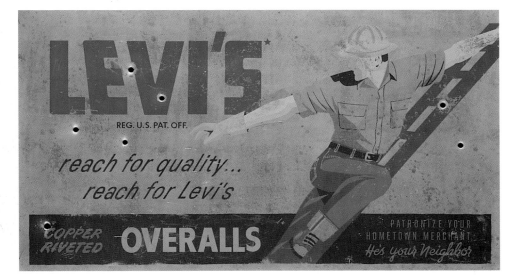

6

1. *Levi's® Heritage Retail Shop featuring archival silhouette man display and metal signage.*

2. *Detail of Levi's® fixture plaque.*

3. *Men's spotlight fixture.*

4. *Detail of product locator signage.*

5. *High capacity fixture.*

6. *Distressed metal signage (complete with bullet holes).*

ZIMMERMANN CROWE DESIGN
90 Tehama Street, San Francisco, CA 94105   415.777.5560   Fax: 415.777.0370

232

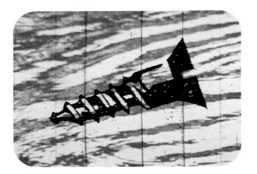

As a part of a trend-related retail merchandising program for Levi's®, ZCD directed and produced several edgy in-store image videos. The videos attract blue jean consumers to the Levi's® area of the store with visuals and music, then encourage multiple sales by featuring Levi's® shirts, Levi's® jackets, Levi's® shorts and Levi's® sweats together with their famous jeans.